PARENTING TEENAGE BOYS FOR PURPOSE

Guiding Godly Young Men to Walk in Charisma, Character, Calling, Life Skills, and Christ-Centered Confidence

Bukky Ekine-Ogunlana

© Copyright Bukky Ekine-Ogunlana 2025 – All rights reserved.

The content contained within this book may not be reproduced, duplicated, or transmitted without direct written permission from the author or the publisher.

Under no circumstance should any blame or legal responsibility be held against the publisher, or author, for any damages, reparation, or monetary loss due to the information contained within this book. Either directly or indirectly. You are responsible for your own choices, actions, and results.

Legal Notice:

This book is copyright protected. This book is only for personal use. You cannot amend, distribute, sell, use, quote, or paraphrase any part, or the content within this book, without the consent of the author or publisher.

Disclaimer Notice:

Please note the information contained within this document is for educational and entertainment purposes only. All effort has been executed to present accurate, up-to-date, and reliable, complete information. No warranties of any kind are declared or implied. Readers acknowledge that the author is not engaging in the rendering of legal, financial, medical, or professional advice. The content within this book has been derived from various sources. Please consult a licensed professional before attempting any techniques outlined in this book

By reading this document, the reader agrees that under no circumstances is the author responsible for any losses, direct or indirect, which are incurred as a result of the use of the information contained within this document, including, but not limited to,—errors, omissions, or inaccuracies.

Published by

TCEC Publishing

TCEC House

England, Great Britain

Dedication

This book is dedicated to our three amazing children and all the beautiful children worldwide who have passed through the T.C.E.C 6-16 years program over the years. Thank you for the opportunity to serve you and invest in your colorful and bright future.

Table of Contents

Introduction: *Raising Young Men in a World That's Lost Its Way* 5

CHAPTER 1: *The Role of Fathers in Shaping Young Men* 8

CHAPTER 2: *Building a Godly Home Environment* 27

CHAPTER 3: *Instilling Godly Values and Character* 33

CHAPTER 4: *Helping Your Teen Son Become Spiritually Alive* 49

CHAPTER 5: *Walking Through the Teen Years Together* 62

CHAPTER 6: *Talking with Your Teen Building Real Connections* .. 82

CHAPTER 7: *Discipline with Grace and Accountability* 87

CHAPTER 8: *Building a Lifelong Relationship with Your Son* 94

CHAPTER 9: *Rooted and Ready Nurturing Calling, Career, Christ, Charisma, and Character in Your Son* 99

CHAPTER 10: *Helping Your Son Build Strong, Healthy Relationships* 114

CHAPTER 11: *Walking with Your Son Through Life's Ups and Downs* .. 126

CHAPTER 12: *Trusting God with Your Son's Future* 136

CHAPTER 13: *Fatherhood That Leaves a Legacy:* 11 Real-Life Lessons from the Frontlines 145

CONCLUSION: *A Legacy Worth Leaving* 219

Please Leave a Review! 222

Other Books You'll Love! 223

Your Free Gift! 227

References 228

Introduction:
Raising Young Men in a World That's Lost Its Way

Raising a teenage boy today feels like building a house in a storm. Every day brings new challenges—screens, culture, shifting values, and constant noise. And in the middle of all that chaos is your son, trying to figure out who he is, who God is, and what his place in the world should be.

If you're reading this as a father—or as a mentor stepping into that role—you know this isn't easy. Life is busy. Work is demanding. Some days, just making it to bedtime feels like a win. Deep talks and spiritual wisdom? Those can feel like distant ideals.

But here's what we can't afford to ignore: **your role in your son's life is crucial as he is becoming a man.**

And he's going to become one with or without your help, but your guidance and influence can significantly shape his development.

That's why this book exists—not to add guilt or more to-dos, but to give you simple tools and biblical wisdom to walk beside your son on his journey toward manhood.

You don't need to be perfect or have all the answers. What your son needs most is your **presence**. A father who shows up. Who loves him enough to guide, correct, encourage, and pray?

Because manhood isn't built on hype, muscles, or money. True manhood is built on **faith**, **humility**, **integrity**, and **strength of character**.

You're not raising a boy for this world to applaud.

You're raising a man heaven will recognize.

Inside these pages, you'll find:

- Real-life advice for connecting with your teen, even when he seems distant

- Biblical wisdom on identity, discipline, and legacy

- Encouragement for when you feel overwhelmed or unqualified

- Simple steps for busy dads and mums who still want to make a significant impact

- Honest stories from other fathers who've struggled, failed, and chosen to lead anyway.

This is a book for **real dads and mums**, not perfect ones.

So, whether you're starting fresh or picking up broken pieces...

Whether your son is five or fifteen...

Whether you had a great dad, a bad one, or none at all...

This journey is for you.

Let's raise sons who understand who they are, *who* God is, and why they're here.

Let's raise godly men who will honour God and make a positive impact on the world.

After reading this guide, please feel free to leave a review based on your findings and how valuable the guide was to you. I would be incredibly thankful if you could take 60 seconds to write a brief review on the platform of purchase, even if it's just a few sentences!

Chapter 1:
The Role of Fathers in Shaping Young Men

"He will turn the hearts of the fathers to their children, and the hearts of the children to their fathers." – **Malachi 4:6**

Dear Father, Mentor, or Guardian,
This chapter isn't just about parenting. It's about **legacy**.
Whether you're a biological dad, stepdad, mentor, spiritual Father, or simply a man who cares, your presence is not just important, it's crucial. In a world of noise, opinions, and distractions, one voice still carries unmatched power in a young man's life: **his father**'s.

Identity Isn't Taught—It's Spoken
Ask most grown men who shaped them most deeply, and you'll likely hear one name: their father. That name is spoken with either deep gratitude… or quiet pain. Why? Fathers do more than name their sons; they **shape their future**, and with that power comes great responsibility.

Reflection Prompt: What kind of man are you shaping with your words today?

Young men today are bombarded by social media, YouTube influencers, and shallow stereotypes of masculinity. But underneath it all, they're asking the same timeless questions:

- Who am I?
- Do I matter?
- Do I have what it takes to be a man?

And here's the truth: no algorithm, video, or celebrity can answer those questions like you can. **Your words are not just words, they are the building blocks of identity.** Your presence brings not just direction, but a sense of purpose.

What Does It Mean to Be a Father?
Being a father isn't just about biology. It's about **intentionality**.

A father protects, provides, and speaks life into his children. He brings calm when the world gets loud. He doesn't just show up—he leads.

Biblical Anchor: Genesis 18:19
"For I have chosen him so that he will direct his children and household after him to keep the way of the Lord..."

God chose Abraham not because he was perfect but because he would **lead**. He passed on a vision, a faith, and a legacy. That's your calling, too.

For today's Father, that means praying with your kids, asking real questions, being emotionally present, and leading by example, not just in public but in private moments that your children will remember forever.

A Tale of Two Fathers

Liam became a dad at 24. While his wife prepared for their new baby, Liam stayed distracted—immersed in games, late nights, and drinking. His son, Theo, grew up emotionally distant, often seeking a sense of identity and purpose through social media influencers.

Then there's **Henry**. A single man in his 30s who started mentoring boys at church. One young man, Jack, had no father. Henry taught him to pray, apply to college, and believe in himself. Years later, Jack said, "I became a man because of a father I never had."

Biology doesn't make a father. **Intentional love does.**

Fathers Impart Identity

Children inherit more than a father's last name. They carry his **Spirit**.

Biblical Example: Matthew 3:17

"This is my beloved Son, in whom I am well pleased."

Before Jesus performed a single miracle, the Father affirmed Him. Why? Because identity comes **before** achievement.

Mike's Story: Mike noticed his teenage son loved to draw. Instead of brushing it off, he bought him a tablet and enrolled in an art course. That same boy now works as a digital artist, using his gift to inspire others.

Words shape destiny. What you say—or don't say—becomes your son's internal voice for years.

"The first words in the Bible weren't for conversation. They were for creation."

Meditation Story: The Night Elijah Cried
(A reflection on the creative weight of a father's words)

Daniel sat at the edge of his son's bed, the soft hum of the night settling into the room like a warm blanket. The glow of the hallway light spilt in gently, casting long shadows on the walls. Just eight, Elijah lay curled up, his face half-buried in the pillow, his shoulders rising and falling with quiet sniffles.

He hadn't said much since getting home from school. Again.

Daniel didn't press. He just sat, present, listening to the silence as if it were speaking.

He remembered being eight, the ache of not being chosen, pretending it didn't hurt, stuffing it all down because "boys don't cry." He remembered how his dad's voice could fill a room, but not always in a way that helped. This memory, this pain, fueled his determination to be a different kind of father to Elijah.

"Toughen up." "Don't act like that." "Get over it."

Words that echoed long after the moment had passed. Words that didn't build—they bruised.

But tonight, Daniel would do something different.

After a while, Elijah mumbled into his pillow, "I didn't get picked again."

"For what, buddy?" Daniel asked softly.

"For the game... at recess. Nobody wants me on their team. They said I'm too slow."

Daniel felt it—that deep father pain—not for the game but for the *story* his son was starting to tell himself: *"I'm not enough."* His heart ached with empathy for his son's struggle.

He placed a hand gently on Elijah's back. "Hey... listen to me."

Elijah didn't lift his head, but Daniel could tell—he was listening.

"I know it hurts. I do. But I need you to know this: You are not what people say today. You're not your speed. You're not the team you didn't make. You're not left out. You are mine. You are loved. You are chosen." His words were a fortress of reassurance for his son.

There was a pause, thick with emotion.

"I mean it, Elijah. Even if you were the last one running in every race, you'd still be first in my heart."

The blanket rustled. Elijah shifted slightly. His breathing slowed.

Daniel leaned in.

"You want to know something else?"

A small nod.

"When God made you... He wasn't chatting. He wasn't making small talk. He was *creating*.

Just like He did at the beginning—when He said, 'Let there be light.' His words didn't just fill the silence. They filled the world with life."

Another pause. A breath.

"And when He made you, Elijah, He didn't rush. He didn't copy. He created. You are one of a kind. And what He made... is really, really good." His voice was filled with pride for his son's uniqueness.

The room felt still like heaven was leaning in.

"Dad?" Elijah's voice broke the quiet.

"Yeah?"

"Can we pray?"

Daniel smiled. Not the kind you put on for show—the kind that wells up from the sacred.

They prayed—not fancy words, just real ones. A father brings the fragile pieces of his son's heart to the One who created both of them.

And as Daniel left, he knelt again beside the bed.

"You're not alone in this, Elijah. Not ever. God's with you. And I am, too."

He kissed his forehead, turned off the light, and entered the hallway.

Later that night, as he sat alone on the couch, Daniel exhaled in the quiet room around him. He hadn't fixed the world. But he had helped shape one.

One where his son wasn't defined by the voices on the playground.

One where his words didn't just react—they created.

And he thought again of the beginning—how God's first words didn't come to make conversation. They came to make *everything*.

So tonight, he whispered to himself, *let there be light*.

And there was.

Toxic Words Leave Long Shadows

A 16-year-old once heard his Father say, "You're useless—just like your uncle." He carried that shame for decades until someone else spoke life one day, breaking the cycle.

Biblical Example : When Fear Carries a Son

Let's pause for a moment. Imagine a little boy—five years old. Still small enough to be carried, still young enough to believe the world is safe. His name is **Mephibosheth**.

One tragic day, news came that changed everything. His Father, Jonathan, and his grandfather, King Saul, died in battle. Grief and chaos swept through the palace like a storm.

His nurse—his caretaker, the woman who likely bathed, fed, and sang him to sleep—heard the news and panicked. Her instincts kicked in: *Get the boy. Run. Now.*

So, she scooped him up in her arms and ran.

But in her fear and desperation, she dropped him.

And from that moment on... **he couldn't walk.**

Not because she didn't love him.

Not because she wanted to hurt him.

But because fear took the lead—and fear doesn't carry gently. Fear can lead us to make decisions that we think are protecting our children, but in reality, they can cause more harm than good. This is a powerful analogy for the impact of our actions and reactions on the young boys in our lives.

"Jonathan, son of Saul, had a son who was lame in both feet… His nurse picked him up and fled, but as she hurried to leave, he fell and became disabled."

—2 Samuel 4:4

That's more than a story from long ago. It's a mirror.

Because here's the hard truth for every Father, mentor, or man who's helping raise the next generation:

You can wound a son without ever meaning to.
Not just with your words.

But with your silence.

Not just with your mistakes.

But with your reactions.

Not just by what you do.

But by what fear do you avoid?

A harsh word in a moment of frustration.

A missed opportunity to say, *"I'm proud of you."*

A cold shoulder when what he needed was your presence.

A moment of correction that came without connection.

These don't always leave visible bruises. However, they can leave boys emotionally limping, unsure of who they are or where they belong.

They may grow taller... but not always stronger.

But Here's the Hope
Mephibosheth's story doesn't end in pain.

Grace stepped in.
Years later, King David asked, *"Is there anyone left in the house of Saul to whom I can show kindness for Jonathan's sake?"* (2 Samuel 9:1)

He remembered his friend. And he remembered the boy.

So David found Mephibosheth and welcomed him—not as a broken burden, but as a family.

He restored his dignity.

He gave him a place at the king's table.

He gave him back a future.

You may be reading this and feeling the weight of your past. Maybe you've dropped your son—through absence, fear, temper, or distraction. Perhaps you carry regret.

Here's the truth:

God still restores.
God still seeks out the broken.

And He still uses fathers and mentors—like you—to lift sons back up again.

Remember, you don't have to be perfect. But you do have the power to choose your presence in your son's life. That's what matters most.

You have to be **present.**

When faced with fear, choose **faith. It's the key to overcoming the challenges of parenting**.

Love overreaction.

Truth over silence.

Let's not carry our sons with fear.

Let's carry them with wisdom.

With gentleness.

With the steady, healing presence of a man who chooses to stay.

Because when you carry a son with love... you help him walk tall again.

Jason: When Fear Sounds Like Protection but Feels Like Rejection

Jason had made himself a quiet promise long ago: *I'll be nothing like my Father.*

He still remembered the feeling—lying in bed as a boy, his chest tight, eyes wide in the dark, waiting to hear if that front door slam meant trouble. His dad was a man of few words and a heavy presence. You always knew when he was in the room, even when he didn't speak. Especially then.

So, when Jason became a father, he told his wife, *"I'm going to do it differently."* And he meant it.

In the early years, he did. He showed up for games. He read bedtime stories. He kissed scraped knees and cheered for scribbled crayon drawings. He wasn't perfect, but he was present.

Then came the middle school years.

Micah, their firstborn, hit thirteen—and hit a wall. Grades slipped. Attitude flared. Motivation vanished.

Jason didn't shout. He didn't storm out or slam doors. But something shifted.

He got tight. Sharp. Demanding.

"You're not even trying."

"You think life is just going to hand you everything?"

"Get your act together—I'm not raising a failure."

He thought he was protecting his son from the real world, toughening him, and raising the bar.

But to Micah, those words didn't sound like love.

They sounded like disappointment.

He started to shrink. Not in stature—but in Spirit.

Dinner became quiet. Conversations felt forced.

Micah smiled less. Laughed less.

He wasn't slamming doors—he was *slipping away*.

One night, Jason walked past his son's cracked bedroom door and heard his voice:

"Nah, my dad doesn't listen. He wants results."

Jason stopped cold in the hallway.

That one sentence—softly spoken, not meant for him—hit harder than any shout ever could.

Because deep down, he knew...

Micah wasn't wrong.

Jason wasn't angry. He was afraid.

Afraid his son would fail.

Afraid of failing as a father.

Afraid of repeating history.

But in trying not to be his dad, he had become someone else: *unreachable*.

And then came the moment he never got as a boy.

He walked into Micah's room and sat beside him on the bed. No speech. No scolding.

Just a quiet, honest, father-to-son confession:

"I've been afraid. I've let that fear push me too hard. But I need you to know… I see you. Not just your effort. You.

And I'm proud—**not** just of what you do, but of who you are."

Micah didn't burst into tears. He didn't leap into his dad's arms.

But he nodded. And that wall between them? It cracked.

A few days later, Micah stayed at the table a little longer.

The silence began to thaw.

Take This to Heart
Fathers, hear this:

You can "drop" your son without raising your voice or hand.

Fear doesn't always look loud.

Sometimes, it looks like cold silence, demanding expectations, and emotional distance.

It wears a mask that says, *"I'm just trying to help."*

But to your son, it might sound like, *"I'll never be enough."*

So don't let fear speak louder than love. Instead, foster an emotional connection that speaks volumes.

Don't trade presence for pressure.

Don't confuse correction with connection.

Your son doesn't need a perfect dad.

He needs a *present*.

He must know he's seen, safe, and deeply loved—*even when he's still becoming.*

You can't control everything he'll face.

But you can shape how he sees himself as he faces it.

That's what fathers do. That's what *you* can do—today. Start by spending quality time with your son, engaging in activities he enjoys. Listen to him without judgment, and let him know you're there for him. These simple actions can make a world of difference in your relationship.

When You Don't Know What to Say, Start Here:
- "I believe in you."
- "I see something special in you."
- "God has great plans for your life."
- "I'm proud to be your dad."

Your Home Is Your First Church
You don't have to preach. Just **live it**.

Biblical Example: Joshua 24:15
"As for me and my house, we will serve the Lord."

Teddy's Example: Teddy, the Quiet Leader
Teddy never forced prayer. But every morning, his sons saw him kneeling in quiet devotion. One day, his oldest son said, "Dad, I start my day like you do now."

Cautionary Tale: One Father said, "I worked hard so my kids could have everything." His son later replied, "We had everything… except you."

The Father Gap Hurts Deeply

Fatherlessness doesn't just create emotional pain. It creates real-life consequences.

Studies show that children without active, present fathers are:

- 4x more likely to live in poverty
- 2x more likely to drop out of school
- At higher risk of depression, addiction, and incarceration

Reflection: Are you **present** in your child's life or just physically around?

Fathers Build the Future

God is a Creator, and fathers reflect that image.

Genesis 4:21 – Jubal

"The father of all who play the harp and flute."

His creativity became his children's legacy.

Take Dylan's story- His son struggled with math, so Dylan crafted homemade wooden games to help him learn. Today, that boy is a high school math teacher. This is just one example of how a father's support and encouragement can shape a child's future.

Fathers **create** space, confidence, faith, and momentum.

Impartation Is the Father's Gift
Genesis 27 – Isaac Blesses Jacob

This wasn't just about words—it was about destiny.

Daniel's Story: Daniel the Builder

Daniel's son loved taking apart gadgets. Instead of scolding him, Daniel said, "I see a builder in you." That boy now designs drones.

Legacy Starts with You

Maybe you didn't have a great dad. Perhaps you didn't have a dad at all.

That's okay. You can **become** one.

You don't have to be perfect—just present.

You don't have to have all the answers—just be willing to listen.

You don't have to fix the past—you just have to start today.

Like Abraham, you can father generations… just by choosing to lead now.

Legacy Challenge

Tonight, write a short letter or prayer to your son. One truth. One blessing. One sentence that speaks life.

Reflection Questions
1. What kind of words are you speaking over your son?
2. What identity do your children carry because of you?
3. What one action can you take this week to connect more deeply?
4. Are you spiritually leading your home or outsourcing that role?

Words for reflection.

A son without a father is like a traveller without a compass.

Be the compass.

Be the voice that brings clarity.

Be the heart that brings healing.

Be the man whose legacy begins—not someday—but **today**.

Chapter 2:
Building a Godly Home Environment

"Unless the Lord builds the house, those who build it labour in vain." — **Psalm 127:1**

You're Not Building a House—You're Building a Legacy
Let's get this straight: building a godly home isn't about having the perfect Instagram family or getting your kids to memorize Leviticus. It's about being intentional. It's about showing up with love, grace, truth, and a bit of grit—day in and day out.

Deuteronomy 6 doesn't say to *preach* the commandments once a week. It says to *live* them—when you sit, walk, lie down, get up all day. Your home doesn't need to be polished; it just needs to be centred on Jesus.

1. Your Home Is Preaching—What's the Message?
Whether you know it or not, your home has a "soundtrack," a spiritual atmosphere, and your kids pick it up. Every Word,

reaction, and silence says something about God, love, identity, and what matters most.

You are not just a provider. You're a spiritual thermostat. You set the tone.

Real Story: Joshua's Quiet Revival

Joshua is not a pastor. He's just a dad who decided to make space for God in his living room. Every morning at 6:45 a.m., he gathers his family. There are no phones. There are no fancy devotionals. There is just a verse, a few thoughts, and a prayer.

At first, it was awkward. The kids fidgeted, and his wife side-eyed the clock, but he stuck with it.

Months in, something shifted. Elijah, his son, asked, "Can I lead tomorrow?" That's when Joshua knew—this wasn't a routine anymore. It was culture. Faith had become part of the house, like the air they breathed.

Now Elijah is praying over his siblings, leading worship, and mentoring younger boys. Joshua didn't just teach his son to read the Bible—he showed him how to live it.

Why It Worked

- **He was consistent** (not perfect—just present).
- **He kept it simple** (no sermons, just real talk).
- **He included his kids** (which built ownership).

- **He prayed by name** (and spoke identity over them).

He wasn't building a habit. He was building a legacy.

The Other Side: Mark's Silent Home

Mark loved his family and provided well, but he figured the "God stuff" was what church was for. He was always busy, and dinners were rare. Spiritual conversations? They never happened.

When his son Tyler asked to pray together, Mark brushed it off. "Maybe later." That never came.

Now Tyler's 17 and distant. His mentors are online influencers preaching rebellion and self-glorification. When Mark finally tried to step in, Tyler said, "Now you care? You're too late."

It wasn't that Mark was a bad dad. He was just absent where it mattered most.

How to Start a Devotion Life at Home (Without Making It Weird)

You don't need a theology degree. Just an open Bible, a willing heart, and five minutes of real talk.

Here's How:
1. **Pick a time** — Morning, night, right after dinner. Keep it short (10–15 min).
2. **Read one verse** — Ask, "What does this mean for us today?"

3. **Invite everyone in** — Let your kids pray, read, or share.

4. **Keep it relational** — Less doctrine, more life.

5. **Speak identity** — End with a blessing over your child. Say their name. Say who they are.

"Elijah, I see strength in you. You don't have to be perfect—just faithful. God's hand is on you, and I'm proud of who you're becoming."

2. Creating a Culture of Love and Respect

Ephesians 6:4 doesn't say, "Be nice dads." It says, "Don't provoke your kids to anger—bring them up in the way of the Lord." That means discipline with love, leadership with humility, and authority with compassion.

Real talk:
- **Listen before you correct.**
- **Validate emotions, even if you disagree.**
- **Create space for failure—without fear.**

The goal isn't obedience. Its connection. Obedience flows from trust.

3. Guard the Gates: What's Entering Your Home?

You're not just raising a son—you're shaping his worldview. What he watches, listens to, and scrolls through forms his theology more than any sermon.

What You Can Do:
- Use **parental controls**, yes—but also **relational controls**. Talk about what he's seeing.
- Ask questions: "What did you think about that video?" "What would Jesus say?"
- Encourage alternatives that grow his creativity, not just his screen time.

You can't control everything. But you can influence the culture of your home.

4. Handle Conflict Like a Man of God

Conflict isn't the problem. How you handle it is.

When your house is full of yelling, sarcasm, or cold silence, your son learns that emotions are dangerous. When it's full of honesty, prayer, and forgiveness, he knows that emotions are a chance to grow.

Model This:
- Pause and pray when things get tense.
- Speak the truth, not just frustration.
- Say, "I was wrong," and mean it.

Conflict is in the classroom. Let your son see what grace looks like under pressure.

5. Let Prayer Be the Glue

Do you want to invite God in? Start talking to Him as a family.

It will feel weird at first. That's okay. Push through. One awkward prayer at a time builds a culture where God isn't a stranger—He's in the family.

"God, help us love each other better today. Be with my son. Lead him when I can't. Amen."

Your kids don't need you to pray perfectly. They just need to hear that prayer is a real thing.

The House You Build Is the Man He Becomes

You don't need to get everything right. You just need to be **present**, **prayerful**, and **anchored in grace**.

Don't just build a house. Build a home where God is welcome, love is normal, truth is spoken, and your son sees Jesus, not just in church, but in you.

Reflection Questions

1. What's one area of your home life that needs more intentionality?

2. How can you handle conflict in a more Christlike way?

3. What's one spiritual habit you want to start with your son this week?

Chapter 3:
Instilling Godly Values and Character

*"Train up a child in the way he should go, and when he is old, he will not depart from it." **-Proverbs 22:6***

Going Deeper Than Good Behaviour

Raising a respectful, well-mannered son is a good goal, but it's not the *ultimate* one. God didn't just call us to raise kids who behave in public. He calls us to shepherd hearts. At the core of godly parenting is helping your son become a young man of character who lives with integrity, humility, courage, and a deep sense of who God is.

This chapter is about how to do just that—not through lectures or perfection—but through presence, example, and Scripture woven into life's everyday moments.

1. What Does Godly Character Really Look Like?

What matters most to God? The heart.
As 1 Samuel 16:7 reminds us, *"The Lord does not look at the things people look at... the Lord looks at the heart."*

Here are some traits we want to build into our sons, not just for Sunday mornings, but for real life:

- **Integrity**: Doing what's right, even when no one is watching.
- **Humility**: Do not think less of yourself, but think of yourself less.
- **Courage**: Standing firm when it would be easier to stay silent.
- **Self-control**: Saying "no" when everything in you wants to say "yes."
- **Kindness**: Choosing compassion, even when it's not deserved.

A Real-Life Example
Joseph was sold by his brothers and imprisoned for something he did not do, yet he never lost his integrity. He honoured God in the dark before anyone saw him in the spotlight (Genesis 37–50).

A Modern-Day Parallel

Michael, a dad of two, noticed his teenage son, Alex, wrestling with peer pressure. Instead of preaching, he got honest. He shared his struggles from high school, the moments he did not stand firm, and when he did. They began reading Proverbs together and having genuine conversations. Over time, Alex gained the courage to make different choices—*his own* choices—with character.

When Your Son Must Stand Alone: Lessons from the Sons of Korah

There comes a moment in every young man's life when he's faced with a choice: blend in or stand up. And sometimes, the hardest part is realizing that standing up might mean going a different way than those he loves—even family.

It is easy to forget, but even in Scripture, not every son followed in his father's footsteps.

In **Numbers 16**, Korah Dathan and Abiram launched a full-scale rebellion against Moses. They questioned God's appointed leadership, stirred up division, and pulled others into defiance. What followed was devastating—God's judgment was swift and sobering.

But tucked quietly into **Numbers 26:11** is this simple, almost hidden line:

"The sons of Korah did not die."

Those few words carry the weight of a thousand choices. These boys—raised in the home of a man who challenged God—**chose differently**.

Imagine the inner conflict: watching your Father lead a rebellion and feeling the pull to stay loyal to your family. And yet, something in them knew: *this isn't the way*. And they dared to step back, to stand apart—even when it cost them.

They didn't follow unthinkingly. They stood with God.

And what became of them? Not bitterness. No shame. But *worship*.

The **sons of Korah** went on to write some of the most beautiful and soul-deep psalms we have in Scripture:

"God is our refuge and strength, an ever-present help in trouble..." (Psalm 46:1)

"Better is one day in Your courts than a thousand elsewhere..." (Psalm 84:10)

Those aren't just poetic words. They are the songs of young men who had seen rebellion—but chose reverence. They had every reason to carry pain, but instead, they carried praise.

As parents, we should have hope.

Your son may one day be in a situation where everyone else—including people he trusts—is making the wrong choice. He may feel the weight of expectations, the confusion of mixed messages, and the pressure to conform. He might even question the values you've taught him.

But if you've taken the time to plant **truth** in his heart, to model **courage** and **conviction**, to root him in **Scripture**—he'll have what it takes to stand.

Even if he must stand alone.

It's because a godly character isn't always loud. It's often quiet. Often unseen. It's when a teenage boy chooses not to laugh at that joke. The moment he walks away from the party. The moment he says, "This isn't right," even if no one claps for him.

That strength doesn't come from rules—it comes from **roots**.

So, don't just raise a rule follower. **Raise a God-seeker.**

So remind your son, gently and often:

Real strength isn't about being liked, followed, or praised. It's not about popularity or being the loudest voice in the room.

It's about being faithful. Even when no one's watching. Even when it's hard. Even when he feels alone.

Let the quiet courage of the **sons of Korah** speak louder than the noise of the world:

Where you come from doesn't have to define where you're going.

Your family history isn't your final story.

Your legacy is not about your past; it's about the One you follow now.

And with God's help on your side—**with your love, prayers, and steady presence beside him—your son can write a different kind of story.**

A story that is marked not by rebellion but by worship.

Not by pressure but by purpose.

A story of courage, character, and quiet strength rooted in Christ. And that's a legacy worth leaving.

How You Can Apply This:
- Share stories of biblical characters—and your own journey.
- Ask your son about his choices and what shaped them.
- Catch him showing godly character and affirm it—big or small.

2. Leading by Example: It Starts With You

"Follow my example, as I follow the example of Christ."
—-1 Corinthians 11:1

Kids don't need perfect dads. They need honest ones, dads who don't just talk about grace but ask for it when they mess up.

When It's Done Well

David wasn't afraid to admit when he blew it. If he lost his temper, he apologized. That taught his son, Ethan, more than a thousand lectures on humility ever could.

When It's Missed

Tom meant well, but he didn't realize how often he shut down his son's feelings. He avoided hard conversations and rarely admitted when he was wrong. Over time, his son stopped opening up altogether.

Try This:

- Apologize when you fall short—it builds trust.
- Be open about the character God is shaping in *you*.
- Invite your son into conversations, not just correction.

3. Letting Scripture Shape Everyday Life

"Impress them on your children... Talk about them when you sit at home and walk along the road..." **—Deuteronomy 6:7**

God never intended Scripture to stay in a church pew. It was always meant for the kitchen table, the car ride, and the bedtime prayer.

Practical Ways to Do This:

- Start mornings with a simple verse or devotional—even 3 minutes counts.

- Talk about how God's truth applies to what's happening at school, in sports, or online.
- Pick a verse a week to memorize together, and talk about what it *means*, not just how to say it.

Single Parent Spotlight:
Sarah, a single mom, used bedtime to share one verse with her son, Liam. He started living it out, showing patience with his sister and kindness at school. It didn't take hours—it just took consistency.

4. Using Consequences to Teach, Not Punish

"The prudent see danger and take refuge, but the simple keep going and pay the penalty." **—Proverbs 27:12**

Discipline isn't about control. It's about *training*. And sometimes, the best way to train is to let a consequence do the teaching.

A True Story
Daniel's son, Noah, kept skipping chores. Instead of yelling or bribing, Daniel calmly said, "We had a fun outing planned today, but since the chores weren't done, we're staying home." Noah learned fast and without bitterness.

How You Can Apply This:
- Let your son feel the natural result of poor choices.
- Talk with him *after* the moment, not just during it.
- Ask: "What do you think God's teaching you through this?"

5. Celebrating Godly Growth

"Encourage one another and build each other up."
—-1 Thessalonians 5:11

Boys Don't Just Need Correction—They Need Celebration.

Sure, boys need guidance when they mess up, but just as much, they need to know when they're getting it right. When your son shows kindness, courage, or patience, *say something.* Let him know who he's becoming matters, and that godly character is worth celebrating.

A Moment That Mattered

Marcus watched his son, Caleb, do something brave—he stood up for another kid being picked on at school.

Later that day, instead of just saying, "Nice going," Marcus looked him in the eye and said,

"That's what a man of God does. I'm proud of you."

It wasn't just a compliment—it was a moment that spoke to Caleb's identity. And it stuck.

Try This:
- Say something out loud when your son shows a glimpse of God's heart—kindness, honesty. Let him know you see it and celebrate it. Those moments matter more than he thinks. Be specific. Let him know his choices matter; as you see the man, he's growing into it.

- Celebrate the effort, not just the result. "You really stuck with Son's, even when it was hard"—goes a long way.

- **Bottom line?** Your words shape your son's view of himself. Use them to build him up.

- Create small moments—notes, hugs, outings—that mark the Spirit's growth.

The Breaking That Built Us
A Story for Every Parent Who's Tried and Felt Like They Failed

Marcus Williams was the kind of dad who meant well. He had a quiet strength, a firm handshake, and a shelf full of Christian parenting books—dog-eared, highlighted, underlined. He attended every game, fixed every broken bike chain, and never missed Sunday service. From the outside, it looked like he was doing it all right.

But inside his home, something was cracking.

His teenage son, Jordan, once all energy and endless questions, had started retreating. First, it was the headphones at the dinner table. Then, the door stayed closed more often than not. His once chatty boy now responded in grunts and shrugs.

Marcus tried to hold the line. No phones at meals. Devotions every Sunday evening. House rules are carved in principle. When Jordan questioned them, Marcus gave the kind of response he thought was righteous:

"Because I'm your father."

Or worse, "Because the Bible says so."

He thought he was training his son in godliness, but somewhere along the way, discipline had drowned out the dialogue. Rules replaced relationships.

Then came *that* Friday night.

Marcus found Jordan sitting alone on the porch, hood up, eyes low, the glow of his phone lighting up his face in the dark. Marcus sat beside him and tried to break the silence.

"You okay, son?"

Jordan shrugged. "I'm fine."

"You sure? You can talk to me."

That's when it came.

"No, I can't," Jordan snapped, pain and frustration in his voice. "You don't *listen.* You just tell me what I *should've* done. You don't even care how I feel."

And then—silence. A gut punch of truth.

Marcus sat there, stunned, throat tight. He didn't even try to defend himself.

He went inside that night, closed the door to his study, and opened his Bible like a man desperate for air. Proverbs 22:6 stared back at him:

"Train up a child in the way he should go, and when he is old, he will not depart from it."

But it hit differently this time.

What if training wasn't about managing behaviour but moulding the heart? What if it looked more like *walking* than *talking*?

The Turning Point

Marcus stood momentarily at his son's door the next morning, praying under his breath. Then he knocked.

Jordan didn't answer, but Marcus walked in anyway. Not as an authority figure. As a father—wounded, humbled, and willing to try again.

"Son," he said, voice low, "I need to say something. And I need you to really hear me."

Jordan turned, unsure.

"I owe you an apology. I've spent more time correcting you than *connecting* with you. I've been trying to shape your behaviour instead of seeing your heart. And that's not who I want to be. That's not who *Jesus* is."

Jordan didn't speak. But he didn't look away either.

Marcus went on. "When I was your age, I gave in to a lot of stuff I wish I hadn't. I did it to be accepted… because no one ever taught me how to stand when it's hard. I didn't have a dad who helped me through those moments. But you do. And I want to be that for you. If you'll let me."

Jordan swallowed. His eyes glistened. And for the first time in a long time, he nodded.

It was the beginning of something new.

The Rebuild

Marcus stopped trying to be the perfect dad. He started being a present one.

He listened more, asked open-ended questions, and told stories from his life—real, messy, redemptive.

Scripture became part of their rhythm, but not in forced devotionals. It came up in car rides, over fries after practice, or during walks when Jordan couldn't sleep. One night, Marcus told him about Joseph— how he held onto integrity when no one was watching—not to preach, just to share.

Jordan asked deep questions like, "How do you say no when everyone else is saying yes?"

Marcus didn't quote a verse. He told Jordan about a business deal he had once walked away from because it would have compromised his integrity. He lost money. But he kept his witness.

Then came the day Jordan stood up for a kid being bullied—not because he was told to, but because something in him had shifted.

That night, Marcus didn't just say, "Well done." He knelt, eye to eye, and said, "That's *what a man of God does. You defended someone weaker than you. That takes courage. That takes character.*"

Jordan stood a little taller after that. His heart was opening—and it showed.

Full Circle

A few months later, during small group, Jordan surprised everyone.

He volunteered to share a devotional.

"I used to think following God was just about rules," he said. "But lately, I'm learning it's more about grace. My dad—he's not perfect. But I've seen him grow. I've seen him apologize. And that made me want to know the God he follows."

Marcus wept that night. Not out of pride. But relief.

He hadn't saved his son.

Grace had.

And he had finally made space for it to do the work.

Final Reflection

Marcus once believed that firm parenting meant strong control. But in the breaking—when his systems failed, and his son's heart cracked—something sacred happened.

He let go.

He listened.

He leaned into the humility of Christ.

And what felt like failure became fertile ground for genuine faith to grow.

He didn't raise a perfect boy.

He raised a faithful one.

And in the end, that's the legacy that lasts.

What Legacy Are You Leaving?

Instilling godly values isn't about raising a perfect kid but growing a *faithful* one. And that starts with us showing up, living it out, and pointing to Jesus in the small stuff.

Your son will learn more from your example than from God's lesson you teach. So walk with him. Mess up and try again. Stay rooted in God's Word. And trust that the seeds you plant—one verse, one conversation, one prayer at a time—*will grow*.

Reflection Questions

1. Which godly traits do you already see in your son? What's your nurturing plan?

2. In what area is God challenging *you* to grow as a father?

3. What's one way you can bring Scripture into daily life? What's this for you?

4. How can you help your son earn from his choices without shame?

5. What's a new way to celebrate your son's character this week?

Chapter 4:
Helping Your Teen Son Become Spiritually Alive

Understanding the Role of the Holy Spirit

The Quiet Battle You Might Not See

It's late on a Friday night. Your son's in his room, the door closed, and headphones on. His phone lights up in the dark every few seconds. From the outside, he seems okay—his grades are decent, he is respectful, and maybe even goes to youth group.

But something feels... off.

Last Sunday, he sat through the church, his eyes distant. When you ask how he's doing spiritually, he says, "I'm fine," or maybe, "I don't know."

And inside, you're wondering: *Is he really okay?*

Is he just going through the motions?

Is his faith even *his*, or is it something he inherited?

If that hits home, you're not alone.

Many teenage boys are aware of God, but they haven't truly *encountered* Him in a way that awakens something profound within. They may follow the routine—church, youth group, Christian-sounding answers—but they're not living in a real relationship with God.

A Modern-Day Herod: How the Enemy Hunts Our Sons

Long ago, King Herod sought to kill a baby named Moses, who would later lead God's people out of slavery. He tried again with Jesus, sending soldiers to stop a child who would change the world. Herod's aim was precise: stop God's plan by destroying the sons.

Herod's tactics have changed today, but the enemy's goal remains unchanged. He's not sending soldiers, but he's hunting your son through pornography, music, entertainment, social media, and the endless pursuit of pleasure. These modern "Herods" don't always look like evil. They wear headphones and screens. They whisper lies of loneliness, worthlessness, and distraction, pulling your son away from his God-given identity and calling.

Just like Herod couldn't physically reach Moses or Jesus, many fathers are called to protect their sons spiritually—from dangers that aren't always visible. This means watching over what enters their hearts and minds, standing guard against the subtle attacks that can cripple their Spirit long before any physical harm.

The battle for your son's soul is real—and urgent. But remember, just as God protected Moses and Jesus, He promises to protect your son, too, especially when you lead him to walk closely with the Holy Spirit, the ultimate Defender and Guide. The Holy Spirit is not just a concept, but a vital presence in your son's life, and your role in fostering his relationship with the Holy Spirit is crucial.

1. Why Spiritual Life Matters More Than Good Behaviour

Let's be honest: being "a good kid" isn't the same as being spiritually alive.

Your son might know all the correct answers, stay out of big trouble, and even talk the talk, but if the Holy Spirit hasn't breathed life into his heart, it's just performance.

It's like tapping someone on the leg who has nerve damage. You touched them, but they didn't feel it.

That's what it's like when a person is disconnected spiritually.

And today's teens? They're up against *a lot*. More noise. More pressure. More temptation. Without a vibrant connection to the Holy Spirit, they're fighting battles they were never meant to fight alone.

You might start noticing:

- **Spiritual boredom** – "Church is boring."
- **Split life** – One way is at church, and the other is at school.
- **Slow drift** – Not rebellion, but a quiet disconnect inside.

2. So... Who *Is* the Holy Spirit, Really?

Let's be real—when boys hear the name *"Holy Spirit,"* it might sound like something out of a fantasy movie. Mysterious. Foggy. Like some invisible ghost drifting through the air. Not exactly someone you'd expect to help with everyday problems—like anxiety, peer pressure, temptation, or trying to figure out who you are.

But here's the truth:

The Holy Spirit isn't a mist. He's not an "it."

He's a **person**. He's **real**. And He wants to walk through life with your son—closer than his breath, guiding him in every step.

When your son begins to know the Holy Spirit, not as an idea but as a friend, it can change *everything*. The Holy Spirit is not a distant figure, but a close companion who wants to walk through life with your son–closer than his breath. Understanding this can help your son develop a more personal and meaningful relationship with the Holy Spirit.

Here's what that looks like:

- **Comforter** – Picture your son curled up in his bed, heart racing after a rough day. Maybe he messed up. Perhaps he's afraid. That's when the Holy Spirit whispers peace—not just a "don't worry about it," but a deep, soul-level calm. The kind of peace Jesus promised—the kind the world can't offer (John 14:16).

- **Convictor** – The Holy Spirit is like a compass always pointing to truth. He doesn't shout or slam us with guilt. Instead, He gently nudges our hearts when we're veering off track. Like a true friend who cares too much to stay silent, He guides us—not to shame us, but to bring us back to what's good, right, and life-giving (John 16:8).

- **Teacher**, Think about how we use Google. We type in a question, and it searches through data to provide us with answers. But the Holy Spirit? He doesn't just scan the internet—**He searches the very heart of God**. And then He brings those profound, eternal truths into our hearts in ways we can understand and live out (1 Corinthians 2:10).

- **Empowerer** – He gives your son courage when he's scared to stand alone. He gives strength when temptations pull hard. He offers words when he doesn't know what to say. The Holy Spirit isn't just power in theory—He's boldness in action. He equips your son to live out his faith in real, everyday ways (Acts 1:8).

But—and this is critical—your son needs to know this:

Lust will lie to him.
Satan will lie to him.
Even his own heart can lie to him.

Jeremiah 17:9 tells us the heart is deceitful above all things. That's why "following your heart" or "doing what feels right" isn't enough. Your son needs something more profound, something unshakeable. **He needs truth.**

And here's the beautiful part:

Truth isn't just a statement. Truth is a Person.
Jesus didn't say, *"I have the truth."*

He said, *"I am the Truth."* (John 14:6)

That means truth isn't just a concept to understand—it's someone we can **know**, **love**, and **walk with**. And it's the Holy Spirit who introduces us to that truth. He doesn't just help us understand Jesus—He helps us truly *know* Jesus.

We relate to the physical world through our senses—sight, sound, touch, taste, and smell. But we relate to the Holy Spirit through a different kind of awareness: the gentle tug in our Spirit, that sudden peace that doesn't make sense, the still, small voice that says, *"Go this way."*

That spiritual sensitivity grows stronger when your son keeps a **clean conscience**—when he stays honest with God, confesses his mistakes quickly, and keeps his heart tender. A soft heart hears the Spirit but unconfessed sins hardens it.

And remember this:

The Holy Spirit is a helper and is not a special reward for preachers or people who seem extra holy. He's a gift Jesus gave to **every believer—including** your son. His presence ensures that your son is never alone on his spiritual journey.

Once your son begins to honestly know the Holy Spirit—not just as a name, but as a friend, a guide, and a constant companion—he won't walk through life alone again.

3. Let's Talk About the "Weird" Factor

Let's admit it: sometimes, talking about the Holy Spirit feels awkward, maybe even too spiritual.

But these conversations matter. And they don't have to be complicated.

Try something like:

"God gave us the Holy Spirit to help us. He can guide us when we feel unsure and give us peace when we are anxious. You can talk to Him, just like you'd talk to me."

Let him *see* you living it out:

- Pause and pray together when facing a decision.
- Play worship music and just sit with it.
- Let spiritual talk be natural, not something forced.

By creating a home where it's normal to talk about the Holy Spirit—without needing to 'have it all figured out'-you're empowering your son to explore his spirituality in a safe and open environment.

- **How to Help Your Son Grow Spiritually (Practically)**

a) Teach Him to Slow Down

In a world of constant scrolling and instant answers, spiritual growth requires something different: stillness.

Isaiah 28:16 says, "He who believes will not be in haste."

Help your son practice being quiet with God, not always to get something, but to be with Him. Sometimes, the silence is where the Spirit speaks the loudest.

b) Walk With Him Through Doubt and Pain

Every teen faces storms—breakups, insecurity, let-downs. Don't just toss Bible verses at him. Be there. Sit in it with him.

Gently remind him:

"Even if you feel nothing, God is still with you. You can be honest with Him."

Joy does come in the morning, as Psalm 30:5 says—but the night can feel long. Walk with him through it.

c) Help Him Connect the Dots

Spiritual moments are powerful, but they need to be grounded in reality.

Encourage him to:

- Write a few lines about what he's feeling.
- Pray out loud.
- Ask simple questions like, "What's this verse telling me about God?"

Help him build a faith that's both felt *and* thought through.

5. Spotting the Signs of Spiritual Life

As your son begins to connect with the Holy Spirit, you might notice:

- **Love** where there used to be anger.
- **Joy** that doesn't depend on good days.
- **Peace** in the middle of anxiety.
- **Patience** when things go sideways.

You might also see gifts show up—encouragement, leadership, wisdom, and other qualities that reflect the character of God.

But stay anchored. Help him avoid chasing emotions or checking boxes. The goal is a *deep*, steady passion rooted in truth.

6. Teach Him to Ask for the Spirit—Daily

Ephesians 5:18 says, "Be filled with the Spirit."

It's not a one-time event. It's a *daily invitation*.

Teach your son:

- You can ask for the Holy Spirit's help every day.
- Staying connected looks like worship, prayer, and simple obedience.
- You're not just meant to survive—you can *thrive*.

That's how spiritual fire is lit—and stays burning.

What Happens When He Comes Alive Spiritually?

You'll start to see it:

- A heart that's tender to God.
- A deeper response is when he feels conviction, more surrender, and less shame.
- Choices are shaped by discernment, not peer pressure.
- Wisdom beyond his years.

This isn't religion. It's a revival in your son's heart.

Higher Ground: Spiritual Perception

As he matures, your son may begin to *experience spiritual feelings* before he can fully understand them. A verse might hit differently.

A sense of peace might settle during prayer. A decision might just" click."

Don't rush these moments. Teach him to:
- Sit with it.
- Pray through it.
- Ask God for clarity and peace.

This is how he learns to walk *in step* with the Spirit, not just near Him.

Pray with Questions—Because God Actually Answers
Prayer doesn't always have to be a polished speech. Sometimes, it's just sitting with God and asking, "Why is this happening?" or "What should I do next?"

We often think we must come to Him with strong, confident, faith-filled declarations. But God isn't intimidated by your questions. In fact, He invites them.

When you ask Him with a sincere heart, you'll be surprised how often He responds, not always with words, but with clarity, peace, and little nudges in the right direction.

God knows everything. Literally *everything*. So imagine what He could show you... If you just asked.

And here's the thing—He does answer. Not always in the way you might expect, but always in the way that's right.

Sometimes, his answers feel a bit like traffic lights:

Green – "Yes. Go for it. This is my will for you."
Amber – "It's coming... just not yet. Be patient."
Red – "No. Not this. Trust Me—I see what you don't."

It's not about getting quick fixes. It's about growing closer to the One who *is* the answer. So, ask the real questions. The hard ones. The ones you're afraid to say out loud.

"God, am I on the right path?"

"What are you doing this season?"

"Why does this hurt so much?"

"What do you want me to learn here?"

He may not say much in the way we expect. But if you lean in, listen, and watch—He'll show you more than you ever thought possible.

Prayer isn't a performance. It's a relationship.

So bring your wonder. Bring your doubt. Bring all of it.

And ask always.
Thoughts: You Can't Force Fire—But You Can Feed It
You can't manufacture a spiritual awakening in your son. Only God can do that.

But you *can* make your home a place where the Spirit is welcome.

Let him see you:

- Waiting on God when answers are slow.
- Worshipping freely, not performing.
- Owning your mistakes.
- Praying with boldness.

Because when the Spirit truly grabs hold of your son's heart, no trend, pressure, or doubt will be enough to shake him.

Reflection Questions for You, Dad

- Am I leading my son toward a real relationship with the Spirit—or just good behaviour?
- When did I last share a real spiritual moment or struggle with him?
- What one thing can I do this week to invite the Holy Spirit more into our home?

Chapter 5:
Walking Through the Teen Years Together

"Don't let anyone look down on you because you are young, but set an example for the believers in speech, conduct, love, faith and purity." - 1 Timothy 4:12

The teenage years can feel like a wild rollercoaster—for both your son and you. It's that in-between time, caught somewhere between childhood and adulthood, where everything seems to be shifting all the time.

Your son is wrestling with big questions, riding waves of changing emotions, and trying to understand who he really is and where he fits in the world.

It's a lot for both of you, but it's also a time full of growth and discovery. These years might come with their fair share of challenges, but they're also full of potential—this is a time when your son can really grow and come into his own, especially in his spiritual life.

As his dad, you're not on the sidelines. You're right there with him. This is your chance to walk alongside him—offering support, sharing wisdom, and showing patience and grace as he figures out who he's becoming. It's not always easy, but it's one of the most critical times in his life for you to be there, and your role in his spiritual journey is not just crucial, it's irreplaceable.

1. Identity: "Who Am I, Really?"

What's going on?

Your son is searching for who he is. In a world that measures worth by popularity, looks, and social media likes, he easily loses sight of his actual value. That's where you come in. He needs to hear—again and again—that his identity is rooted in something much more profound: he is fearfully and wonderfully made (Psalm 139:14) and deeply loved by God.

Real-life inspiration:
A Moment Like Samuel's

Remember the story of **young Samuel**? He was just a boy—maybe around your son's age—when he first heard God speak to him in the quiet of the night. But at first, Samuel didn't recognize the voice. He thought it was Eli calling him from the next room. It took a few tries, but Eli, the older and wiser mentor, gently helped him understand:

> *"The next time you hear that voice, say, 'Speak, Lord, your servant is listening.'" - **(1 Samuel 3:9)***

What a moment. A small, unsure boy in the stillness of night whispers a prayer that changes everything.

And here's the beautiful part:

You get to be that "Eli" for your son.
You can help him learn how to recognize the voice of God—not by shouting or trying harder, but by **quieting the noise** around him. You have the power to show him how to pause before reading his Bible and say, *'Lord, speak to me.'* You can also encourage him to pray regularly, read the Bible, and participate in church activities to foster a deeper connection with God.

Let him know it's okay if it doesn't feel dramatic. Sometimes, the voice of God feels like a soft idea that won't go away or a verse that suddenly feels *just for him.*

Sometimes, a deep peace settles inside him or a gentle warning that says, *"Not that way."*

Whether reading Scripture, lying in bed after a hard day, or walking through something confusing or painful—**he can hear God's voice**.

Not in a spooky way, but in a real, personal, Holy Spirit way.

Because the same God who called out to Samuel still speaks today. And the same Spirit who whispered to prophets, apostles, and believers throughout history—**now lives inside your son.**

Once your son starts to know the Holy Spirit—not just hear about Him, but truly *know* Him—

he'll never walk alone again.

Cautionary tale:
Absalom, David's son, sought to establish his identity through rebellion and ultimately caused harm to himself and others. Trying to build an identity on outside approval or defiance doesn't hold up for long.

How you can help:
- Ask about his dreams and interests—just listen.
- Help him plug into a church group where he can belong.
- Remind him that his worth doesn't change, no matter what the world says.

2. Peer Pressure: The Need to Fit In
What's going on?
Friends Matter—More Than We Sometimes Realize
Friendships are a big deal for your son. The desire to fit in with his peers and be accepted can run deep; sometimes, that pressure can pull him in the wrong direction. Romans 12:2 gently reminds us not to conform to the world but to let our lives be shaped by God's truth instead. That's a powerful calling, but let's be honest—it's not always easy, especially when your son just wants to belong.

A Quiet Kind of Courage

Picture this: a young guy, far from home, surrounded by people who don't believe what he does or live the way he's been taught. That was Daniel. He could've blended in, gone with the flow—but he didn't. He didn't argue or try to prove a point. He simply stayed true to what he knew was right. This story can really encourage your son—it shows that even when things get tough, he can hold on to what he believes in.

Daniel didn't need to be loud or dramatic to be strong. His strength was quiet, steady, and came from a deep trust in his faith. That kind of strength can make a lasting impact. That kind of courage still speaks today. It shows your son that he doesn't need to make a scene to be strong. Sometimes, the bravest thing to do is holding firm to your beliefs, even when no one else is holding on to it.

A Gentle Caution

Now, think about Saul. He started off well, but somewhere along the way, he got more focused on what people thought of him more than what God wanted. His need for approval ultimately led him astray. It's a quiet warning: when we care more about fitting in than staying faithful, we can lose our way. Helping your son understand this now can save him heartache later.

How you can help:
- Walk through a few "what-if" situations together so he's ready when peer pressure hits.

- Encourage friendships that help his faith grow.
- Remind him often that doing the right thing is worth it, even when it's hard.

3. The Emotional Rollercoaster
What's going on?
Riding the Emotional Waves

During these years, your son's emotions might feel like a rollercoaster—laughing one minute, silent or upset the next. It's not just mood swings; it's his way of dealing with everything he's feeling. And that is okay. Ecclesiastes 3:4 reminds us there is a time for everything—crying, laughing, being angry, and finding peace

A Real-Life Example:
Real and Honest Like David

David called a man after God's heart and was not afraid to feel deep. He did not hide his emotions or pretend everything was fine. Instead, he brought it all to God—his joy, fear, anger, and sorrow. The Psalms are full of those raw, honest prayers. David shows us that bringing our emotions to God is not just okay—it's actually one of the healthiest things we can do.

A Quiet Caution

Then there's Cain. He felt angry, too, but he let it fester instead of working through it or bringing it to God. And that anger grew into something dark and destructive. His story reminds us that when we ignore or suppress strong emotions, they don't just disappear—they often manifest in hurtful ways.

What This Means for You and Your Son
Help your son see that his emotions aren't wrong or something to hide. They're a part of life, and God cares about every one of them. Let him know it's safe to talk, feel, and bring it all to the One who understands.

What You Can Do:
- Be a safe space for your son—someone he knows he can talk to without fear of being judged or "fixed."

- Let him see how you handle your emotions. Talk openly about your struggles and what helps you through them.

- Teach him simple, faith-centred ways to cope, such as prayer, journaling, or just taking a deep breath and checking in with God.

4. Sexuality: Navigating the Tough Stuff
Let's Talk About It
Puberty can feel like a total whirlwind — physically, emotionally, and mentally. It's entirely normal for your teenage son to begin having questions about sex, attraction, and all the changes happening inside of him. And honestly? The world around us is filled with confusing, mixed messages, especially regarding big

topics like this. That's why, as parents, we're called to show up with honesty, kindness, and care.

Following God's way isn't just about rules or limits—it's about embracing a way of living. It's about helping our kids find true peace, wholeness, and a life that really satisfies them.

When Scripture, like 1 Corinthians 6:18, calls us to turn away from sexual temptation, it's not meant to shame or scare anyone.

It's about caring, protecting and not punishing them.

It's really an invitation to choose a path that leads to freedom, not deep regret.

Our job isn't to lecture or judge but to stand beside them—

to create a safe space where honest, caring conversations can happen, where they feel free to ask questions, wrestle with doubts, and find their own way in their own time.

At the heart of it all, what truly matters is God's way, always rooted in love.

And it's in that love that real fulfilment, healing, and peace are found.

A Story of Quiet Strength

Take a closer look at Joseph's story, and you will see a man who chose to step away and honour God. His quiet courage says so much without needing words to explain it. Did he like it, may be but he did feared God and the love of God constrained him. He was willing to face whatever came his way because of his convictions.

Standing firm doesn't always have to be loud or dramatic—often, it's about showing up with steady, consistent actions. He didn't hesitate or try to argue when temptation knocked at his door. He just made the right choice, no questions asked. Sometimes, real strength isn't loud or dramatic—it's found in being steady. In holding firm, even when the pressure is high.

True courage often looks like quietly holding on to what's right, even when it's easier to give in.

Then there's Samson. He had incredible strength but kept pushing past God's boundaries—testing limits and making riskier choices over and over.

His story reminds us that power without wisdom can fall apart. Strength without surrender just is not enough.

There is a great significant about learning to stay grounded—being strong *and* willing to let go, being firm *and* faithful.

In the end, those choices caught up with Samson in a big way. His story serves as a potent reminder, that ignoring God's guidance can have serious consequences.

How You Can Be There for Him and not waiting for the 'perfect moment' to start these talks — begin early and keep the conversation flowing naturally over time. Your commitment to these ongoing conversations is a powerful way to show your engagement and support.

Be real about how movies, music, social media, and friends shape what he thinks about sex and relationships.

Make your home a place where your teenage son knows he's safe—safe to ask hard questions, wrestle with doubts, and speak honestly without fear of being shut down or judged.

Be the steady presence who listens when he opens up.

The quiet strength beside him when he's struggling.

The gentle guide who offers wisdom—not lectures—when he's ready to hear it.

And through it all, gently keep guiding him back to this truth:

God's plan is always rooted in love.

Even when life feels heavy or confusing, when nothing makes sense—that love hasn't disappeared.

It's still here. Still holding him. Still worth leaning into.

You don't need perfect words or a grand speech.

What matters most is your steady presence. Your consistent support and guidance are invaluable to your teenage son, making him feel important and valued.

The quiet way you show up.

The way your love says, *"You're not alone. You don't have to carry this all by yourself."*

Sometimes, that's the clearest reflection of God's love he'll ever see.

And remember, it's not about having *one* big, awkward, high-pressure "talk."

It's not about having all the correct answers.

It's about showing up—again and again.

In the little moments that don't seem significant at all:

the car rides when he barely says a word,

the late-night snacks when the day is finally quiet,

the casual check-ins that say, *"I'm here if you need me."*

That's where trust begins to grow.

That's where walls come down.

That's where hearts start to open—slowly, safely, in their own time.

Keep showing up. That's what matters most. It's about being there for him daily, having honest, caring conversations, and showing patience and grace.

Faith: Helping Him Stay Rooted

What's really happening?

Your son is growing up fast, and these years are crucial for his faith—this is when it either takes root or starts to drift. Proverbs 22:6 reminds us that how we guide our kids can shape the paths they will walk later. The spiritual foundation you help build today could be what carries him through out life's most challenging moments down the road, instilling a sense of hope and optimism in you as a parent.

A Real-Life Example

Think of Timothy in the Bible. He didn't grow into a strong man of faith by accident—he had Paul walking alongside him, encouraging and teaching him along the way. That kind of steady, intentional guidance will make the difference.

When the Mask Came Off: A Teen's Turning Point

Sunday mornings always followed the same rhythm in Daniel's house: wake up, dress up, get to church. His parents never missed a service. Daniel didn't either, not because his heart was always in it, but because it was expected of him. He smiled, nodded at the correct times, sang the worship songs, and even helped in the media booth when asked.

On the outside, he looked like every parent's dream teenager: respectful, active in church, and good grades. But on the inside, Daniel was a storm no one saw coming.

He had a secret.

Actually, two.

Lying had become second nature. At first, it was small: "Yeah, I finished my homework," or "No, I didn't see your text." But over time, it grew into a shield—a way to cover the guilt he carried.

Because the other secret was even more on his mind: sexual sin.

It started online. Curiosity turned into a habit, which became an addiction. Then came real-life compromises—texting, touching, and slipping past boundaries he once promised never to cross.

He hated it. Every night, he would lie in bed and whisper, "God, I promise I'll stop." But the promises were empty, and he no longer believed in himself.

"What's wrong with me?"

"I'm the church kid. I'm not supposed to be this messed up."

"If they knew the real me, they'd be ashamed."

Daniel was living in defeat. As long as Jesus had not truly come into his life, sin reigned in him. He had no power to stop it, like a door left open for lions to walk in and tear apart his soul. Every day, he was being mauled spiritually—and he couldn't shut the door. But all of that was about to change.

A Divine Interruption

One Sunday morning, everything changed.

The sermon wasn't flashy. In fact, it felt like the pastor had read Daniel's private journal. He spoke about the prodigal son, shame, hiding, and the love of the father who runs to the broken.

Daniel's heart pounded.

"They have no idea."

"God, I'm tired. I can't do this anymore."

"I don't want to fake it for one more day."

Then came the altar call.

"If you're here," the pastor said gently, "and you're carrying sin, you think God can't forgive... if you're tired of pretending and want to come home... Jesus is waiting. Come."

Daniel's legs moved before he made the decision in his head. He walked past the rows. The weight in his chest and the years of silence came crashing down. Tears poured from his eyes as he knelt.

And then... peace.

Not thunder. Not lightning.

Just peace.

For the first time in years, Daniel wasn't hiding.

"God, I'm sorry. I need you. I can't fix myself, but I believe you can."

Something shifted that day—not just emotionally but spiritually. Jesus came into his life for the first time, and sin lost its dominion over him. Just like a door once left open to lions, it was now slammed shut—and locked.

The evidence that Jesus came into him was simple yet powerful: sin no longer had dominion over him. He could now live above it. "For this reason, the Son of God was made manifest to destroy the works of the devil" (1 John 3:8). That's precisely what happened in Daniel's heart.

Formation Through Fire

Daniel didn't become perfect overnight. But now, he was free.

Before this turning point, Daniel had a great deal of theoretical knowledge. He knew scriptures, could quote memory verses with ease, and was the kid who won Bible quizzes. But it was all cerebral, stored in his mind, never formed in his heart. Church attendance, polished behaviour, even a good reputation—none of it could give him victory.

His youth leader in church had introduced him to fasting, and although it was not required, he voluntarily chose to fast on Wednesdays. He skipped breakfast and ate a snack at 10:30 during the school break. After a few weeks, he pushed himself to skip breakfast and wait until lunch at 12:30. A month later, he was holding out until after 3:30. Eventually, he began breaking his fast at 6 p.m.

It wasn't about performance—it was about desperation. As he waited on God, he noticed a shift. Grace was increasing. His mind was clearer. His Spirit was stronger. He began to realize that the way out of strongholds was through death and resurrection—a dying to self and rising in the strength of Christ.

He started meeting with a youth leader who lived a quiet but powerful life. This mentor taught him something that stuck:

"Daniel, when you're tempted to show off, like with prayer, fasting, or giving, hide it. Let God reward that in secret.

But when you're tempted to hide, like with sin, confess, and repent, to bring it into the light. That's where healing lives."

Daniel began to walk in truth. He prayed—really prayed. He installed accountability apps. And he told the truth, even when it was hard.

But behind Daniel's transformation was something invisible: intercession.

His youth leader wasn't just offering advice. He had a secret life with Jesus. Like Elijah would go to Mount Horeb to pray, the youth leader would pray for his teens. His quiet life was loud in the Spirit.

Because fundamental spiritual transformation doesn't occur solely through good preaching. It's not just about what's said on the stage—it's about the labour in the prayer closet.

With just a sentence, Elijah declared rain would stop, but he went up the mountain to give birth to that reality. He bent down, head between his knees, and prayed like a woman in labour. He travailed because certain things must be spiritually delivered.

Just as Elijah sent Gehazi to repeatedly check the sky, Daniel's youth leader persisted in prayer until he saw signs of change. That's what spiritual midwives do. They labour until Christ is formed.

A Life Made New

Daniel eventually sat down with his parents. He confessed everything.

There were tears and awkward silence, but there was also grace. They hugged, prayed, and began healing process together.

Today, Daniel shares his story boldly. He tells other teens:

"Don't let the church clothes fool you."
God's not looking for perfect people—He's looking for *honest* ones.

And the beautiful truth is that He's still in the business of transformation. Every single day.

A gentle reminder for parents:

Your teen might show up at church, smile nicely, sing the songs—and still be quietly falling apart inside.

Don't assume that showing up means they're okay inside them.

External obedience doesn't always mean internal peace.

Ask the more profound questions.

Create space for honest conversations—not just correction, but connection.

Lead with compassion, not control. And when words fall short, *pray.*

Your love, your listening, your faith—it all matters more than you know.

Keep showing up. God's not done writing their story.

Because when Jesus truly comes into a teenager's life, sin loses its power. And when He is formed in them through prayer and discipleship, a new creation is born.

One altar call might be the visible moment. But behind every transformation is often a midwife in prayer—a parent, a pastor, a youth leader, or a friend, bent low in spiritual travail, helping birth the life of Christ in another.

That's the unseen battle.

That's the real work which changes everything.

A Word of Caution

A Gentle Reminder from the Past

Think about the Israelites—after seeing miracles and feeling God's goodness so clearly, they still began to drift away. It didn't happen overnight or because they stopped believing all at once, but because they stopped remembering.

It's a gentle warning for us, too: even a strong beginning in faith can fade if we don't keep coming back to God regularly.

That's where your presence matters more than you might realize. You're not just raising your son—you're helping him build roots that will hold, even when life gets hard.

What You Can Do:
- Set aside a few minutes once or twice a week for family devotions—it doesn't have to be long or formal.

- Encourage him to plug into a youth group or a small circle of friends who share his love for Jesus.

- Most importantly, let him see your faith lived out in how you speak to others, handle stress, pray, and love.

- Faith isn't just taught—it's caught. And your example is one of God's most powerful tools in your son's life.

Reflection Questions

- How can you affirm your son's God-given identity this week?

- Are there ways you can help him handle peer pressure with more confidence?

- How can you create safe, judgment-free moments for open conversations about feelings and sexuality?

- What parts of your faith journey can you share to encourage him?

A Father's Prayer for His Son

"Father God, You know my son better than I ever could. Guide me to walk beside him with wisdom and grace through these challenging years. Guard his heart from the lies that try to shape him. Give him the courage to stand strong and a deep desire to follow You. Help me be the dad he needs so that he can become the man you created him to be. In Jesus' name, Amen."

Chapter 6:
Talking with Your Teen Building Real Connections

"Let your speech always be gracious, seasoned with salt, so that you may know how you ought to answer each person."
— Colossians 4:6

Closing the Communication Gap

Talking to your teenage son can sometimes feel like decoding a secret language. One moment, he's distant or gives short answers; the next, he might snap or shut down completely. But underneath it all, most teens want to connect—they don't always know how or feel safe enough to do it.

As a dad, you play a huge role here. Communication isn't just about talking; it's about building trust, showing you get him, and making your home a place where he can be himself. This chapter shares simple, practical ideas rooted in biblical wisdom to help you bridge that gap and keep the conversation flowing.

1. Be Fully Present

It's easy to be in the same room but distracted—checking your phone, thinking about work, or zoning out. Your son notices when you're not there, making him feel ignored or unimportant.

Try this:

Put your phone aside when he's talking—give him your full attention.

Make eye contact, nod, and show you're engaged.

Ask open-ended questions like, "What was the best part of your day?" or "What has been on your mind lately?"

Why it matters:

Remember Job's friends? They didn't have all the answers, but they showed up and sat quietly with him (Job 2:13). Just being there speaks louder than words, Sometimes.

2. Instead of just asking, **"How was school?"**—which often gets a one-word answer like *"Fine"*—try asking questions that open the door to a real conversation. The goal is to invite your child to share what they *felt*, not just what they *did*.

Ask things like:

- "What was the best part of your day?"
- "Did anything make you laugh today?"
- "Was there a moment you felt proud of yourself?"

- "Did anything happen that made you feel frustrated or confused?"

- "Who did you spend the most time with at recess/lunch?"

- "What's something you wish had gone differently today?"

These kinds of questions gently go deeper. They help kids feel seen—and more willing to share what's going on inside, not just the surface-level stuff.

Try questions like:

- "What was the toughest part of your day?"

- "How do you feel about everything changing around you?"

- "Is there something you wish you could talk about but don't know how?"

These show you care about his honest thoughts and feelings, not just surface stuff.

3. Listen More Than You Speak

James 1:19 says, "Be quick to listen, slow to speak." When your son talks, resist offering advice or solutions.

How:

- Let him speak his mind without interruption.

- Repeat what you hear: "Sounds like school's been really stressful."

- Accept his feelings, even the small or silly ones.

Jesus listened first, like with the woman at the well (John 4), then responded with kindness and understanding.

4. Create a Safe Space for Vulnerability

Teen boys often worry about being judged or misunderstood. You can help by being calm, open, and encouraging.

Try:

1. Don't rush to fix things or criticize.
2. Share some of your own struggles or mistakes (age-appropriate) to show it's okay to be vulnerable.
3. Praise him when he opens up: "I'm proud of you for telling me that."

Think of the father in the Prodigal Son story—he welcomed his son back with love and no judgment (Luke 15).

5. Respect His Privacy

Your son needs room to figure things out on his own. Finding the balance between giving him space and staying involved isn't always simple, but it's really important.

Here are a few things that can help:

a. Talk openly about privacy and set clear boundaries together so you both know what to expect and respect.

b. Let him know you're always there—no pressure, just open doors whenever he's ready.

c. Stay connected through everyday moments not trying to dig into everything.

God gives us free will and gently guides us. Giving your son space helps build trust.

6. Work Together — Avoid Power Struggles

Teens often resist authority. Instead of battles, try teamwork.

Try this:

1. Show empathy first: "I get why this frustrates you."

2. Make rules and consequences together so he feels heard.

3. Focus on how the situation can help him grow rather than just punishing him.

Jesus encouraged questions and learning with his disciples—that's the kind of approach that works.

Reflection Questions

- How can I be more present and focused when my son talks?

- What questions will help him open up more?

- How can I respect his privacy while staying connected?

- How can I turn disagreements into chances to work together?

Chapter 7:
Discipline with Grace and Accountability

"For the Lord disciplines the one He loves, and chastises every son whom He receives." — **Hebrews 12:6**

Let's be honest—discipline is one of the most complex parts of parenting, especially when your son is a teenager. It's not just about laying down rules or handing out consequences. It's about helping him grow into a responsible, mature, godly young man. Discipline isn't about control or punishment. It's about guiding him with love and grace while holding him accountable so his heart and character can develop.

In this chapter, we'll explore how to discipline in a way that builds trust, reaches his heart, and strengthens your relationship.

1. Start with the Heart: What's Really Going On?
Discipline isn't just about fixing behaviour—it's about understanding *why* your son acted the way he did. Think about King David. After his big mistake with Bathsheba, the prophet

Nathan helped him see the real problem in his heart. The real change came from deep inside, not just surface-level fixes (Psalm 51).

Here's a real example:
Michael noticed his son's grades slipping and saw that he seemed withdrawn and moody. Instead of jumping to punishment, he sat down and really listened. It turned out his son was struggling with anxiety. Together, they found help and support, which made a significant difference—not just in school but also emotionally.

What *not* to do:
John punished his son for his bad grades without trying to understand what was really going on. It pushed his son away and made things worse.

Try this:
- Ask gentle, open questions like, "What's been hard for you lately?"
- Listen without interrupting or trying to fix things right away.
- Help your son put words to his feelings and understand what's behind them.

2. Set Clear, Consistent Boundaries
Teenagers often have been found to do better when they know what's expected and what happens if they don't follow the rules. Proverbs 22:6 reminds us to guide children with explicit instruction.

Good example:

Sarah and David agreed on a clear curfew for their son. When he came home late, they stayed calm and followed through with the consequences they had discussed beforehand. Because they were consistent, their son learned to take responsibility and trusted that when they said something, they meant it.

What *not* to do:

Emma kept switching the rules and the punishments for her daughter, Linda, which left her feeling confused and frustrated because she never knew what was really expected of her.

Keep this in mind:

- Be open and honest about the rules and what will happen if someone breaks them. Make sure the consequences fit the situation and feel fair to everyone involved.

- Stick to your word—don't keep changing the rules or making exceptions that confuse your son.

3. Discipline Out of Love, Not Anger

Discipline should come from a place of love and care, not frustration or Anger. Ephesians 6:4 encourages us not to provoke children but to discipline them with love.

Good example:
Lisa's son lied about his whereabouts, instead of getting angry, she calmed down and explained why honesty matters, which opened a positive conversation.

What to avoid:
Tom yelled and punished his daughter harshly after she broke curfew. His Anger created fear and distance instead of understanding.

Helpful tips to use:
Pause and take a deep breath before you respond.

Keep your tone calm and focus on your son's actions, not who he is.

And always remind him that you love him no matter what happens.

4. Teach Accountability: Let Him Own His Choices

Learning to take responsibility is a big part of growing up. As Galatians 6:5 states, we are responsible for carrying our own load.

A good example:
Alex missed a deadline for a school project. Instead of jumping in to fix it, his parents encouraged him to talk to his teacher and figure out a plan. That way, Alex could learn from his mistakes and make things right.

What *not* to do:
Jake's parents blamed the teacher when he failed a test and demanded a retake, taking away his chance to learn from his actions.

How to build accountability:
- Ask your son to think about how his choices affect others.
- Help him come up with solutions or ways to make things right.
- Resist the urge to rescue him from every consequence.

5. Show Grace and Forgiveness: Heal and Move Forward

Discipline is not where all things end — it's actually where healing and connection begin.

Colossians 3:13 reminds us that forgiveness is key. Just as God forgives us, we're called to forgive those we love.

A real-life moment:

When Correction Builds Connection

After Maria corrected her son for being disrespectful, she didn't just end the conversation there. Later, she took a quiet moment to sit with him—not to lecture, but to remind him how deeply she loved him. They talked honestly about how they could listen to each other better and handle things differently next time. That small, loving gesture brought them closer and helped build real trust between them.

What to Watch Out For

Mark, on the other hand, kept bringing up his son's mistakes—even after they had already talked about them. Instead of helping, it made his son feel ashamed and distant. Over time, it created more space between them, making it harder to rebuild trust and truly move forward.

Remember:

. Once you have talked things through, be quick to forgive—don't let the mistake hang over him.

. Say something reassuring, like, *"I love you, no matter what."* Those words go a long way.

. Gently encourage him to take something from the experience and keep growing—it's all part of the journey.

Reflection Questions

- How do I usually discipline my son? Do I focus more on his behaviour or on understanding what's behind it?

- What can I do to make my discipline more consistent, loving, and full of grace?

- How will I help my son learn to take responsibility for his actions?

When you blend grace, clear boundaries, and accountability, discipline becomes more than obedience—it becomes a way to guide your son toward real maturity. Keep love at the centre, and remember that discipline is about care, not control.

Chapter 8:
Building a Lifelong Relationship with Your Son

"A friend loves at all times, and a brother is born for adversity." — **Proverbs 17:17**

The Journey That Keeps Growing

Parenting doesn't just pause or slow down when your son becomes a teenager—in many ways, it's when the real journey begins. These years are a unique opportunity to lay down a foundation of trust, respect, and love that will carry you through all the ups and downs ahead. As your boy grows into a young man, you'll notice your role changing — from the protector who keeps him safe to a mentor who guides him and, eventually, to a friend he can lean on.

1. Be the Example He Can Look Up To

Kids watch us closely — more than they listen to our words. How you live your faith, show kindness, handle mistakes, and treat others speaks volumes.

Think about Paul and Timothy—Paul didn't just see Timothy as a student. He called him his "true son in the faith" (1 Timothy 1:2). That shows how powerful it is to lead by example, not just by words.

In daily life, it's like a Daddy who stays calm and kind, even when things aren't easy. Without saying much, he deliberately and quietly shows his son what patience and compassion truly mean.

2. Make Time That Truly Matters

Life gets crazy busy, but making time for your son is one of the most valuable things you can do. Whether you jump into something he loves or have a simple heart-to-heart, those moments create a lasting connection.

Try this:

- Plan regular hangouts or small traditions that are just for the two of you.
- Jump into what he loves, even if it's not your thing.
- Create a space where he can share honestly without fear of judgment.

3. Move from Boss to Trusted Guide

As your son gets really older, he will want more than just rules — he'll want someone who really listens and can turn to for advice without feeling like he's being bossed around. This is a significant change. It's about shifting from telling him what to do to having honest, real conversations where he feels truly heard.

Tips:

- Invite him to share what's on his mind, big or small.

- Offer advice only when he asks for it — sometimes, just listening is enough.

- Celebrate his wins with him, and be there to catch him when things don't go as planned.

4. Speak Life Through Encouragement

Words matter — a lot. Tell him when you see him trying hard, being kind, or handling challenging situations. Let your son know you see and appreciate *who he is*, not just the things he achieves. Encouraging him in this way helps build his confidence and reminds him that he's valuable just as he is.

Ways to encourage:

- Share specific things you admire about him — the little things showing you honestly see him.

- Tell him how proud you are of the young man he's becoming, even when he's still figuring things out (because nobody gets it all right at once).

- Remind him that he has unique gifts and a special purpose that God has carefully placed in his life — gifts only he can share with the world.

5. Respect His Growing Independence

Letting your son make choices—even mistakes- is a big part of helping him grow into a responsible adult. Trusting him shows you believe in him while staying ready to support him when he needs you.

How to do it:

- Give him age-appropriate responsibilities.

- Guide him gently without controlling every step.

- Keeping communication open will show him that he can always come to you.

6. Grow Together Spiritually Through Prayer

Praying together isn't just about asking for things but building a bond rooted in deep faith, honesty, and vulnerability.

Try this:

- Set regular times to pray about what you're thankful for and what you need guidance on.

- Share what you're learning about God and how it's helping you.

- Encourage him to develop his own personal relationship with God.

Reflection Questions

- How are you showing the values you want your son to live by?

- What small ways can you create more meaningful time together?

- How can you support his independence while staying connected?

- How often do you use encouraging words to lift him up?

- What spiritual habits can you share to grow closer?

By doing these things, you're not just raising a son, building a lifelong friendship and guiding him toward becoming a confident, faith-filled man.

Chapter 9:
Rooted and Ready
Nurturing Calling, Career, Christ, Charisma, and Character in Your Son

---

"The glory of young men is their strength, but the splendour of old men is their grey hair." — **Proverbs 20:29**

Walking Together into Manhood

Raising a teenage boy is like trying to steer a boat through a fierce storm. The world your son is growing up in can feel like a storm—pressures from friends, constant distractions from phones and screens, and a culture that keeps changing the rules. Some days, it might feel like you're both just treading water, doing your best not to sink. But here's the good news: **you don't have to have it all together**. Your son doesn't need a perfect parent—he needs **you** to show up with love, grace, and a willingness to walk alongside him. What your son needs more than anything is your **presence**—your desire to walk alongside him with wisdom, love, and grace as he makes his way through the beautiful yet messy journey of becoming a man.

Being a parent to your son isn't just about ensuring he knows how to cook, drive, or balance a budget. Those things matter—but what matters even more is **who he's becoming**. Your real job is to shape his heart, to help him begin to understand why he's here, and to anchor him in a faith that can carry him through the hard stuff life will eventually throw his way. Because when the storms come—and they will—it's not just the skills that will hold him steady, but the strength of his character and the depth of his walk with God. He doesn't need a list of rules or a bunch of "do's and don'ts"—he needs a **vision for his future**, a heart rooted in Christ, and a character that will keep him steady through whatever life throws at him.

In this chapter, we will walk through five key areas to help you raise a son who's not just getting by—but growing into the man God created him to be. A young man who's:

- Rooted in his calling
- Confident in whatever career path he chooses
- Anchored deeply in Christ
- Able to influence others with healthy, humble charisma
- And grounded in solid, Christ-like character

And threaded through all of it? **The real-life skills**—practical, emotional, spiritual—that will help him stand tall in the world, not just survive it. Because we're not just raising boys. We're raising future men of courage, purpose, and faith.

1. Calling: Helping Him Hear God's Whisper

What It Means:
Your son's calling isn't just about what job he'll one day have or what title he might carry. It's deeper than just a job or a plan—it's about who he's becoming. His calling is like a thread gently woven into God's bigger story, and it doesn't all come into view immediately. It comes to light slowly—through those still moments of awe, the hard seasons, and the steady steps of growing up. When God speaks to you, His voice reveals your purpose. No man can reveal your purpose. It's not about a future job title; it's about discovering his purpose and learning to follow God's voice one step at a time—even when the way forward feels unclear. At the heart of it all is that deep, quiet joy that makes you feel inside, "This is exactly where I'm meant to be."

Make room for stillness: In a world that's always busy and loud, help him find those little moments of calm—away from screens and distractions. Times when he can slow down, take a breath, and catch God's quiet, gentle voice. These aren't just pauses; they're little sacred spaces where clarity begins to take root and quietly grow.

Ask questions that stir his soul: Instead of pushing him toward a path, guide him gently with questions that help him dig deep. Try asking things like, "What breaks your heart?" or "What do you love doing that lifts others?" or "What do you think God created you to bring into the world?"

Ease the pressure: Reassure him that he doesn't have to figure it all out today. Discovering your calling is like unfolding a map slowly—not a one-time lightning bolt. Let him know it's okay to take small steps and make a few detours along the way.

Build life skills around reflection: Teach him how to journal—not just his thoughts but also his prayers and ideas. Show him how to spot patterns in his passions and strengths. Help him learn to weigh decisions using both clear thinking and quiet prayer. These tools will serve him well for a lifetime, no matter where he's headed.

Story to Inspire:
Angela, whose son Luke is naturally quiet, shared, "He's never been one to seek the spotlight. But one evening, he said something that stuck with me: 'Maybe God made me serve others, like Joseph.' That moment changed everything for us.". We stopped trying to push him forward and instead started celebrating the quiet strength he shows behind the scenes."

Try Saying:
- "What do you think God made you good at?"
- "When do you feel most alive?"

- "If you could solve one problem in the world, what would it be?"

Life Skills Spotlight: Self-Awareness & Discernment
Help him build emotional vocabulary and reflection habits—tools to help him understand his inner world and make faith-aligned decisions. Encourage journaling, goal-setting, and time for solitude, even if it's just ten minutes a week. These are sacred, formative practices.

Six Sons, Six Journeys: How Fathers Helped Their Sons Discover Their God-Given Purpose
Every son's path to purpose is a winding journey—full of trial, discovery, and quiet nudges from the Holy Spirit. For dads, it's really about showing up, paying close attention, and gently guiding their sons as they discover their purpose.

Let's look at six real-life stories:

1. Daniel – The Unexpected Teacher

What His Father Did:
- Encouraged discipline by finishing his engineering degree.
- Noticed how Daniel lit up when mentoring others.
- Suggested tutoring as a "low-risk experiment."
- Prayed during moments of career confusion.

Life Skill Integration:
- Daniel learned to **communicate**, plan lessons, and manage different personalities—skills that benefit all professions.

2. Ethan – The Fixer Who Found His Calling

What His Father Did:
- Built him a garage workshop.
- Took him to air shows.
- Connected him with a Christian engineer.

Life Skill Integration:
- Ethan learned **hands-on problem-solving**, **design thinking**, and **collaboration**—critical skills in any technical or creative field.

3. Noah – The Driven Visionary

What His Father Did:
- Had his budget for a family trip.
- Read Proverbs together to discuss money and ethics.

Life Skill Integration:
· Taught **financial literacy**, **generosity**, and **stewardship**—skills he now uses in his personal life and profession.

4. Josiah – The Builder of Dreams

What His Father Did:

- I gave him sketchbooks to capture his ideas.
- Connected him with mentors in construction.

Life Skills Gained:

Josiah learned spatial reasoning, how to present his ideas clearly, and the discipline of refining his work—embracing feedback and improving his designs over time.

5. Malik – The Artist with a Listening Heart

What His Father Did:
He asked Malik, "How did that make you feel really?" encouraging him to reflect deeply. He also gave him a Scripture journal, helping him weave his faith into his art.

Life Skills Gained:
Through this, Malik developed emotional intelligence and empathy, learning to express himself in ways that connect very deeply with others—skills invaluable in caregiving, ministry, or any role where listening and understanding are essential.

6. Levi – The Storyteller with a Shepherd's Heart

What His Father Did:
Levi's father recognised his gift with words from an early age. He laboured to sharpen his gift. He took him to a Christian writers' workshop, opening a door for creative and spiritual growth. At home, he gently invited Levi to lead family devotions—giving him a safe space to practice sharing truth with both humility and heart.

Life Skills Gained Through these intentional moments, Levi didn't just grow as a writer or speaker—he became a compassionate leader. He was deliberately taking time to grow his gift, diving into different cultures to broaden his perspective and deepen his understanding of the world around him. His experience that was nurtured skills in communication, teaching, and spiritual guidance, shaping both his voice and his confidence in leading and establishing others with wisdom and grace

7. Career: Focusing on Vocation

A career rooted in faith goes beyond simply earning a living. It's about stepping into who God made you to be—using your skills, passions, and opportunities to serve others and reflect His character in everyday life.

Encourage your son to see his future work not just as a job, but as a meaningful way to live out his faith. Whether he's fixing things, teaching, designing, or leading, his work can be a reflection of Christ and a response to God's calling. A job pays salary, but work pays gives reward. He can make money through a job and use it to fund his assignment. It's not about status or salary—it's about purpose.

How You Can Help
- Give him a chance to explore different paths—whether through job shadowing, internships, or simply spending time with people in a variety of roles. Real-life experience can spark unexpected interests.

- Talk often about what success really looks like. Help him see that being faithful in his work matters more than chasing titles or applause.

- Keep reminding him of who he is in Christ will always matter more than what's on his résumé. His worth isn't tied to a job—it's rooted in something far deeper and more lasting.

Life Skills for the Workplace:
- **Time Management**: Teach him to plan a day, use a calendar, and meet deadlines.

- **Communication**: Practice interviews and teach him to write a professional email.

- **Work Ethic**: Give him real tasks with honest feedback, even at home.

Real Life Example:
Jason took his son Micah to meet a Christian engineer, a missionary doctor, and a music producer. "I wanted him to see that ministry doesn't just happen at church—it happens wherever you bring Jesus with you."

Ask Him:
- "How could you use your gifts to help others, no matter your chosen job?"

8. Christ: Keeping Jesus at the Center

What It Means
The most crucial relationship in your son's life is his connection with Jesus Christ. This goes far beyond just showing up at church—it's about knowing Jesus deeply and experiencing His presence in everyday life.

How You Can Help
- Let him see what genuine faith looks like—not perfection, but honesty and grace.
- Pray together, even if it feels awkward at first.

Look closely at how Jesus loved, led, and lived, letting His example guide you every step of the way.

Life Skill: Building Spiritual Habits

Encourage simple, meaningful habits, such as writing down one Bible verse each day, pausing to pray before making big decisions, or tuning in to God's voice through music or the stillness of nature. These simple habits become steady anchors—quiet, daily moments that help us stay rooted and grounded, no matter what life brings.

A Mom's Moment

Lisa, mom to 17-year-old Jonas, shared, "We began praying together for just five minutes before bed. At first, it felt a bit awkward—but now, he's the one who turns to me and says, 'Mom, do you want to pray?'"

Sometimes, the small, faithful steps open the most oversized doors.

9. Charisma: Stewarding the Spark

What It Means

Charisma isn't just about charm or being the loudest in the room—it's a quiet spark, a natural ability to draw others in. Some kids are born with that magnetic presence, the kind that makes people listen and lean in.

If your son has that spark, your role isn't to dim it—it's to help him steward it well. Teach him that charisma isn't for self-promotion but for serving others. It's about leading with humility, living with integrity, and using his influence to point people toward what's true, good, and grounded in God's love.

Charisma is influence. It's a spark God gives—**not to shine for ourselves** but for others.

How You Can Help:
- **Affirm his influence** and voice.
- Teach him to use charisma to **serve, not impress**.
- Help him build **inner confidence**, not dependence on external validation.

Life Skill: Interpersonal EQ
- Practice making eye contact, listening without interrupting, and giving thoughtful compliments. These soft skills are the currency of leadership.

Practical Tip:
Charisma is like fire—it can warm or burn. Help him choose warmth.

Challenge Him:
"Make three people feel truly seen this week. Let's talk about how that felt."

10. Character: Building What Lasts
What It Means:

Character is who he is when no one's looking. It's the hidden root system that holds everything else together.

How You Can Help:
- Talk about **integrity** in everyday moments.
- **Let him fail** and help him learn.
- **Model repentance** when you mess up.

When He Messes Up, Walk Him Through:
- "What happened?"
- "What do you think God says about this?"
- "What can we learn from this?"
- "How do we move forward?"

Life Skill: Decision-Making with Wisdom
- Teach him to pause, reflect, ask for input, and seek God before acting.
- Help him see failure not as shame but as part of the process.

Teach Through Stories:

Use people like Joseph, Daniel, and even David—not to glorify perfection but to highlight God's power in imperfect men.

Seeking God in Complex Situations: Practical Wisdom for Parents

Taking Your Mind Along: The Power of Focused Prayer

Getting distracted is easy, but learning to bring your mind back to prayer gently can help you hear God more clearly.

The Spirit's Role: Aligning Heart and Mind

When your heart and mind are aligned, you're more likely to recognize God's direction for your son and you.

Seeking God's Face: A Continuous Conversation

Seeking God isn't a one-time event. It's not about getting it perfect—it's about finding a rhythm. Prayer becomes a conversation, a quiet space where peace settles anxiety, and clarity slowly rises out of confusion.

Practical Steps

- Focus your thoughts when you pray—don't rush.
- Bring both your heart and your mind into it.
- Wait for peace; don't make decisions out of panic.
- Talk openly with your son about what you're hearing from God—let it be a shared journey.

Thought

Your son doesn't need you to have it all together.

He needs roots—and readiness.

Roots that go deep in Christ.

Readiness to step into life with courage and purpose.

He needs your prayers, patience, presence, and willingness to **teach life with love**.

Keep walking with him.

Keep listening.

Keep believing.

Because God is growing something substantial in him, it all starts with what you plant today.

Chapter 10:
Helping Your Son Build Strong, Healthy Relationships

"As iron sharpens iron, so one person sharpens another."
— Proverbs 27:17

Why Relationships Matter So Much Today

Let's be real—growing up today looks much different than it did for us. With so much life happening through screens, genuine, face-to-face relationships can feel like a lost art. But real connection still matters—maybe more than ever.

As parents, one of the most powerful things we can do is help our sons build healthy, strong, and rooted-in-faith relationships—the kind that helps them grow into the man God's calling them to be. And the best place for him to learn that? Right at home, watching you.

1. The Power of Real, Godly Friendships

Think about David and Jonathan's friendship for a moment. These two were not just friends who shared laughs or fought side by side. Their close bond was something very rare—it wasn't just closeness, it was sacred. It was built on deep trust, loyalty, and a shared faith in God.

When David's life was in danger, Jonathan didn't back away. He stood with him, even when it was very risky. It wasn't easy—but to Jonathan, love and faithfulness mattered more than comfort or safety (1 Samuel 18:1-4).

They weren't just friends for the good times. They showed up for each other when everything was falling apart. Jonathan believed in David's calling—so much so that he stood up for him, even when it meant going against his own father because he loved him.

That kind of friendship they both had goes beyond connection—it's soul-deep. It reminds you who you are when everything else feels shaky. It's rare, but when you find it, it can change your life.

Now imagine a teenage boy like Alex. He's not perfect—none of us are—but he's trying to walk with God. And he's got a few close friends who are doing the same. They don't just text memes or play video games (though they do that, too). When Alex is overwhelmed, doubting himself, or feeling like he's slipping, these friends show up when life gets heavy. They remind him who he is and, more importantly, who he is. They pray with him. They speak the truth to him. They help carry his burdens.

Then there's Jake. At first, it didn't seem like a big deal. A new group of friends. A little more freedom. But these friends didn't care about God or direction—they cared about fun, status, whatever felt good at the moment. Jake didn't plan to walk away from his values. But over time, bit by bit, the noise of that crowd drowned out the quieter voice of faith. His grades slipped. His family felt distant. His sense of who he was started to blur.

It didn't all fall apart at once. Slowly, the wrong friendships pulled him off course. That's the power of who we let speak into our lives—for better or worse.

How to help your son find solid friendships:
- Encourage him to get involved in places where genuine connections can happen, such as church youth groups or Christian clubs.

- Let him *see* what real friendship looks like in your life.

- Talk with him about what makes a good friend: trust, accountability, shared values, and someone who brings out his best.

2. Helping Him Stand Tall When Pressure Hits

Remember Daniel and his friends? They refused to compromise their faith, even when it meant standing alone (Daniel 1:8). That kind of courage takes practice and support.

Take Michael. When offered alcohol at a party, he remembered what his dad taught him and said no. He didn't just avoid trouble—he earned respect. Then there's Liam, who gave in to fit in. It cost him—not just his grades but his confidence.

How to prepare your son to stand firm:

- Talk openly. Role-play situations so he doesn't get caught off guard.

- Remind him often: his value doesn't come from fitting in but from being loved by God.

- Let your home be a judgment-free zone where he can talk honestly, even when he messes up.

3. Navigating Relationships

Honest Conversations Between Fathers and Sons

When Paul told young Timothy to treat women "as sisters, with absolute purity" (1 Timothy 5:2), he wasn't just giving a religious recommendation — he was offering a counter-cultural call to integrity in a world full of shortcuts, confusion, and counterfeit love.

As a parent raising a son today, you're not just dealing with phones and feelings — you're walking with him through a culture where dating can feel like a sprint with no finish line, where being liked matters more than being wise, and where heartbreak can come faster than healing.

This isn't a time to stay quiet. This is the time to lean in.

Let's step into three living rooms. Three sons. Three fathers. Three very different stories point to the same truth: **Your voice matters more than you think.**

4. The Father Who Got It Right: Mark and Ethan

Mark wasn't a perfect man. He had a past — scars, regrets, the kind of stuff you'd rather not talk about. But he made a choice early on: *his silence would not be inherited.* So, he opened up to his son, Ethan, not with lectures but with honesty.

One cool fall evening, after tossing the football around, Mark and Ethan sat by the fire pit. The orange flames danced in the fading light, and the smell of burning wood hung in the air.

"Son," Mark said, voice steady but warm, "this world will offer you a hundred versions of love. Most of them are fakes — loud, flashy, fast. But what kind of love does God give? It's different. It's slow, steady, and full of honour."

Ethan listened—not because Mark was some kind of expert but because he was real. Over time, they had deep talks about emotions, sex, boundaries, and identity. Ethan learned how to think clearly when his feelings were strong.

So when Ethan met Mia, he took it slow. They built a friendship. They laughed, served together in youth ministry, and supported each other's dreams. Months later, they began dating. Years later, they walked down the aisle—not as strangers in love but as best friends who built something worth keeping.

Key Takeaway:
Start early. Be honest. When your son trusts your voice before the emotions hit, he's more likely to turn to you when they do.

5. The Father Who Got It Wrong: Darren and Ryan

Darren showed love as he had been taught: work hard, provide for, and protect. He ensured the fridge was stocked, the car had gas, and the lights stayed on. But he stayed silent regarding emotions, girls, or God. He figured his son would just "figure it out" like he had.

So Ryan did. He learned from TikTok and locker room talk. He fell fast and broke even quicker. Each relationship started with sparks and ended with silence. Every breakup came a deeper ache and more questions he didn't know how to ask.

One night, Ryan came home late. His eyes were red, and his hoodie hung low over his face.

Darren looked up from the couch, the TV still glowing in the background. He felt the moment hanging there, fragile.

"Maybe... maybe you should slow down next time."

Ryan didn't look up. Just muttered:

"Yeah. Thanks, Dad. That's really helpful now."

The silence that followed was deafening. Darren sat there, feeling like he missed something big. And he had.

Key Takeaway:
Silence speaks — and not always the message you hope for. If you don't talk to your son about love, sex, and relationships, someone else will. And they may not love Jesus.

6. The Father Who Tried—but the Son Chose His Own Way: Daniel and Caleb

Daniel did his best. He was intentional — he prayed with Caleb, brought him to church, and talked openly about love and dating. Some conversations were clumsy. Others felt forced. But Daniel showed up, and Caleb knew it.

Still, Caleb had a fire in him. He was sharp, charming, and headstrong. He wanted excitement, the thrill of being pursued and praised. To him, rules felt like chains.

So when he met "her," he didn't listen to the quiet warnings. He dove in fast, deep, and blind. The relationship turned toxic, with arguments, manipulation, and pressure. By the time it ended, Caleb was broken.

One night, he sat on his bedroom floor — blinds closed, phone off, heart in pieces. The silence was loud. The guilt was heavier than his chest could carry.

Daniel knocked. Gently.

He walked in with no judgment in his eyes, just love. He didn't stand over him — he pulled up a chair.

"You don't have to say anything," Daniel said softly. "I just want you to know I'm here. And I'm not going anywhere."

Caleb didn't speak that night. But something shifted.

Over the next few weeks, he began to pray again—not with fancy words—just raw honesty.

"God... I messed up. I thought I knew better. I hurt her, I hurt me, I hurt You. I'm unsure how to resolve this issue. But please... fix me."

The wounds didn't disappear overnight. But healing came—slowly, quietly, like spring after a brutal winter.

Then, something unexpected.

During an apprenticeship in a new town, Caleb ran into someone he hadn't thought of in years — **Elise**, the girl next door growing up. She was quiet, thoughtful, never flashy. He hadn't given her much attention back then. But now... something was different.

He prayed. This time, not for what *he* wanted, but for what *God* wanted.

"Lord, if this is from You, I'll wait. I'll do it right this time. Lead me."

And He did.

They started talking—slowly, like friends. They laughed again and shared stories. This time, there was no rush—just peace. Months later, with his father's words echoing in his heart, Caleb pursued Elise with intention, prayer, and purity.

What started in pain, God turned into purpose.

Key Takeaway:
Your patience, presence, and prayers can bring him home even when your son strays. Grace doesn't guarantee perfection — but it opens the door for redemption.

Practical Wisdom for Guiding Your Son

- **Start with God's truth, not just house rules.** Show your son that the Bible isn't about restrictions but protection. God's design is rooted in love, not fear.

- **Encourage friendship before romance.** Help him see that attraction may spark the fire, but friendship keeps it burning.

- **Have the awkward talks.** Don't wait for the perfect moment — create it. Conversations about sex, boundaries, and respect are too meaningful to delay.

- **Connect him to mentors.** Sometimes, another voice — a youth leader, uncle, or older teen — can speak the truth in a way he'll hear.

- **Model it.** How you treat your spouse, coworkers, and the women in your life teaches your son how to love.

A Word to Parents

Your son isn't just wrestling with feelings — he's becoming a man. A man who will one day lead, love, and make choices that echo for generations. Don't shrink back.

Be present. Be prayerful. Be real.

While culture shouts confusion, **you can whisper clarity**—one honest, grace-filled conversation at a time.

7. Keeping the Family Connection Strong

Jesus told the story of the prodigal son, and the father's love in that moment says it all—no matter what, family is where love waits (Luke 15:20).

Look at Lucas and his dad. Every week, they set aside time for dinner and real conversation—phones off, hearts open. Those moments built a bond that remained strong throughout the teenage years. Tyler's family, though, rarely talked or connected, and he often felt like he was on his own.

How to keep your family close:
- Make space for regular connection—meals, walks, games, even just checking in.

- Be a safe place—someone your son can come to without fear of judgment.

- Let love lead. Even when discipline is needed, let grace come first.

- Include time for prayer, faith conversations, or reading Scripture together.

8. Modelling the Kind of Relationships You Want Him to Have

Jesus didn't just *talk* about love—He showed it, washing His disciples' feet as an act of service (John 13:14-15). Our sons learn most by watching how we treat the people in our lives.

Think of David, a dad who consistently speaks kindly to his wife and listens with patience. His son notices. Then there's Mark, who lets anger control him at home. His son notices that, too.

As a parent, your example matters:
- Show what respect, kindness, and humility look like in your relationships.

- Don't just react when conflict arises; show how to resolve and repair it.

- Be honest and consistent. Let your words and actions line up.

Reflection Questions:
- Who are your son's closest friends, and are they encouraging him to be his best?
- How can you help prepare him for moments of peer pressure?
- What do you want him to believe about dating and love, and are you showing that in your own life?
- How strong is your connection with your son right now, and how could you strengthen it?
- What are *you* learning in your relationships that your son needs to see?

Wrapping It Up

Helping your son build healthy, Christ-centred relationships is one of the greatest gifts you can give him. These relationships will influence the man he becomes—how he loves, leads, and lives out his faith.

Be intentional. Keep showing up. And remember, you don't have to be perfect—just present.

Chapter 11:
Walking with Your Son Through Life's Ups and Downs

Seeing Challenges as Chances to Grow

A Fresh Take on James 1:2-3:
Joy in the middle of pain? That's a tough ask. But what if joy isn't just about feeling happy? What if it's about holding onto peace, hope, and a quiet confidence—even when life gets hard? Because the truth is, trials are part of life. And for your son, they might come in the form of school stress, broken friendships, failure, or moments when he just doesn't feel good enough.

It's in those exact moments that he needs you—not just to give him advice, but to walk beside him. Your presence, your prayers, your unwavering love will be the anchor he holds onto when the waves feel too strong. You're not just there to fix the storm. You're there to show him that faith is still possible *in* the storm.

Biblical Inspiration:

Think about Joseph who was not just as a Bible character, but as a real teenager who was kept for an example for today's teenager. When he was Just 17 years old. Still trying to figure out who he was. Still dreaming big, maybe a little naïve, but he was full of hope.

And then—everything shattered.

The people who should have protected him, his own brothers, turned on him. Not in a small way. They didn't just argue or freeze him out. They sold him. Like an object. Like he didn't matter. Can you imagine that kind of betrayal? The kind that doesn't just hurt—it breaks something deep inside. The people he trusted most decided his life was worth nothing.

That doesn't just bruise your heart. It leaves scars.

Being thrown into a pit, trafficked into slavery, sent off to a foreign land—alone and afraid—wasn't just a change in location. It was a tearing away of everything familiar, everything safe. Joseph must've cried. He must've questioned everything. *Why would God let this happen? Where is He now?*

And yet, somehow, in the middle of that pain, Joseph didn't lose himself. He kept going. He kept choosing integrity. He held onto this quiet, stubborn belief that his story wasn't over. That God hadn't forgotten him—even if it felt like everyone else had.

That's not the kind of faith you wear on your sleeve. That's the kind of faith that's forged in heartbreak.

Joseph's story isn't just about rising to power. It's about holding on when everything falls apart. It's about trusting that even when people let you down, God is still working. That what others meant for harm... God can still use for good.

But Joseph didn't let it break him. Somehow, even in the confusion and pain, he held onto the belief that God was still with him. He didn't have all the answers—but he trusted that God wasn't done writing his story. And in time, that trust turned ashes into influence. Joseph's story shows us something we don't always want to hear—but desperately need to know: sometimes, it's in the hardest, messiest, most painful parts of our lives that God does His deepest work. When everything feels like it's falling apart, when we're asking "Why this?" or "Why now?", that might be the very place where God is shaping us—quietly, gently, into the people we're meant to be. Not in spite of the struggle, but through it all..

Real-Life Story:
Leo thought his world had ended when he didn't get into college. It felt like a dead end, like he wasn't good enough. But instead of rushing to fix it, his dad gave him something even more valuable: time. He encouraged Leo to pause, to serve, to explore. That year changed Leo—it helped him find what he was passionate about and gave him clarity he never expected. What looked like failure

became a doorway to purpose. That happened because his dad believed in the long game, not just quick fixes.

Practical Ways to Support Your Son:
- Help him see that obstacles are not stop signs—they're stepping stones.
- Share stories like Joseph's when life feels unfair or unclear.
- Create a home where it's safe to not be okay—where there's no shame in fear or failure.
- Pray with him. Pray for strength, for joy, and for the kind of faith that doesn't break under pressure.

Handling Pressure from School and Career

Biblical Inspiration:
Daniel was just a young man, suddenly thrown into a world that didn't look anything like home. New culture, new rules, new expectations—and a whole lot of pressure to blend in, to go along with the crowd, to let go of what he believed just to survive.

But he didn't cave.

Even when it would've been easier to stay quiet or compromise just a little, Daniel chose to stay true to who he was. He held onto his faith when everything around him pushed him to let go of it. And that took real courage—not just the loud, heroic kind, but the quiet, daily kind that says, *"I know who I am, and I know who God is."*

Daniel's story reminds us that doing the right thing might not always be what everyone is doing , it may not make you popular—but it makes you grounded. It's proof that integrity means more than approval. And when life feels like a pressure cooker, his life is a reminder: God sees it. God honors it. And you're never alone in it.

Real-Life Story:
Jamie was at that crossroads so many young people face—trying to figure out what to do with his life while the pressure kept piling up. Friends were talking about careers in finance, tech, medicine—the kind of paths that promise stability, status, and a big paycheck. And everyone just assumed he'd follow the same route. It would've been the easy choice. The safe one.

But something inside Jamie didn't sit right.

The more he thought about it, the more he felt pulled in a different direction—toward people, toward purpose, toward ministry. It didn't make sense on paper. It wasn't flashy. And it definitely wasn't what most people expected of him. But it felt honest. It felt like *him*.

Still, it was scary.

That's when his dad stepped in—not with pressure, but with presence. He didn't try to talk Jamie out of it. He just listened very carefully. Asked the right questions. Prayed with him. And shared stories from his own life about choosing meaning over money. A couple of mentors echoed that support too, helping Jamie realize that it's not about impressing people—it's about being faithful to what God placed in your heart.

So Jamie took the leap.

And no, it wasn't always easy. But every time he saw lives touched, hope restored, or someone feel seen for the first time—he knew he'd made the right choice. Choosing purpose over popularity wasn't just brave. It was beautiful. And it changed everything.

Practical Ways to Help:
- Talk with your son about his *gifts*, not just grades or goals.
- Help him explore dreams that match his identity—not what the world says he "should" do.
- Keep reminding him: Success isn't about status—it's about faithfulness.

Dealing with Failure and Setbacks

Biblical Inspiration:
Peter blew it—badly. He denied Jesus at the moment it mattered most. But Jesus didn't shame him or shut him out. He welcomed him back, forgave him, and gave him a mission. This was really soothing. That kind of grace changes everything. It says: "Your worst moment isn't your final chapter."

Real-Life Story:
Allen poured his heart into a business that failed. He felt like a total failure—lost and ashamed. But his dad didn't give him a lecture. He shared his own painful stories, showing Allen he wasn't alone. That honesty gave Allen courage to try again—and eventually, to succeed.

Practical Ways to Support:

- Be open about your own stumbles—it gives your son permission to be real.

- Help him find meaning in failure—it's a teacher, not a tombstone.

- Remind him that his worth isn't tied to success. His identity is secure in Christ who is living inside.

Supporting Him Through Relationship Struggles

Biblical Inspiration:
David and Jonathan's friendship was real, loyal, and safe—This was a gift in a complicated world. Their story shows how important strong, supportive relationships are, especially when life gets rough.

Real-Life Story:
Archie was bullied and felt completely alone. His confidence vanished. But his dad stepped in—not just with words, but with

action. He got involved, helped Archie connect with a church youth group, and slowly, things changed. Archie found belonging again—and his spark returned.

Practical Ways to Support:
- Be a safe place for him to talk about friendships or dating—listen more than you speak.
- Talk about the value of forgiveness, loyalty, and healthy boundaries.
- Let him see those values in how you treat people every day in your relationship.

Walking With Him Through Doubts and Questions
Biblical Inspiration:

Thomas doubted—and Jesus didn't scold him. He showed up, with scars still visible, and said, "See for yourself." That moment reminds us: God can handle our questions. And He meets us right where we are.

Real-Life Story:
Bailey hit a wall in college. Faith felt distant, full of questions with no answers. But his daddy did not panic. He stayed close as much as he could, listened, offered resources, and prayed with him. And slowly, Bailey began to see that faith isn't about having no doubts—it's about trusting anyway.

Practical Ways to Help:
- Let your son ask hard questions without fear.
- Share books, podcasts, or mentors who've wrestled with faith and come out stronger.
- Pray *with* him, not just for him—and let him hear you trust God even when answers aren't clear.

Final Thought:
Being a dad in today's world isn't easy. But it's sacred work. You're not just raising a boy—you're walking beside a young man learning who he is in God's story. There will be pain. There will be questions. But if your son knows he has a father who sees him, listens to him, and walks with him—that may just be what gives him the strength to keep going.

Practical Tips:
- Encourage your son to ask questions honestly and without fear all the time.
- Explore the Bible or faith resources together.

Reflection Questions for You:
How can you help your son see tough times as part of God's bigger plan, not just obstacles on his way now?

What can you do to support him as he chases his dreams while staying grounded in his faith?

How do you encourage him to pick himself up and keep going when he falls or messes up?

How will you walk alongside him when he faces challenges with friends, dating, or relationships?

- How can you create a safe space where he feels comfortable sharing his doubts and questions without fear of judgment?

Why This Chapter Matters:
- It blends Bible stories with real-life examples you can relate to.
- Offers practical steps you can start using today.
- Comes from a place of understanding — parenting isn't perfect, but walking together makes all the difference.

Walking with your son through life's most challenging moments strengthens your bond and builds a foundation of faith and trust that lasts a lifetime.

Chapter 12:
Trusting God with Your Son's Future

A Legacy of Faith, Not Control

"'For I know the plans I have for you,' declares the Lord, 'plans to prosper you and not to harm you, plans to give you hope and a future.'" — *Jeremiah 29:11*

"And we know that in all things God works for the good of those who love Him, who have been called according to His purpose." — *Romans 8:28*

Let's Be Real

Parenting a teenage boy isn't for the faint of heart. One moment, he's joking with you and laughing in the kitchen; the next, he's closed off in his room, headphones on, barely saying two words. You love him more than you can even put into words—but sometimes you catch yourself wondering:

- Is he going to be okay?
- Have I done enough?
- What if he makes choices I can't protect him from?

If you've ever been awake at night worrying, second-guessing, or praying with a shaky heart—you're not alone. Every mum and every dad has been there. And here's some relief: you don't have to have it all figured out. You're not raising your son on your own. **God is holding his future—even when you can't see it.**

Letting Go of *Your* Plan

We all have hopes for our kids. It starts small—like what sports they'll play or if they'll like reading—and then it becomes bigger: what they'll become, who they'll marry, the kind of life they'll build. But sometimes, the hardest (and holiest) thing we do as parents is let go of *our* plan so they can step into *God's*.

A Dad's Story:

John always pictured his son wearing a white coat with a stethoscope. But his son had a different heartbeat—music. At first, John pushed back. But then he chose to listen. And what he saw next was life: his son came alive. There's something powerful in letting go—and trusting that God knows what He's doing.

Try This:

- Check in with your expectations: Are they from God or your fears and dreams?

- Talk to God honestly—about your hopes *and* your anxieties.

- Let your son try and fail. That's not wasted time—it's where growth lives.

Helping Him Hear God for Himself

We want our sons to grow up wise, strong, and grounded. But most of all? We want them to know how to hear God's voice—because life will throw all kinds of noise at them.

A Real Moment:

Michael was being pulled in every direction by friends, trends, and pressures. His dad didn't give him a list of rules. He kept asking: *"What do you think God wants for you?"* That one question slowly became a guiding light for Michael.

Try This:

- Let your son see *your* process—how you pray and wrestle with decisions.

- Don't underestimate the power of praying together, even if initially awkward.

- Encourage relationships with mentors who live with quiet faith and purpose.

When You Don't Know What to Say (or Do)

Let's be honest: there are moments when we have no idea what we're doing. You want to give the perfect advice or have all the answers... but you don't. And that's okay to know.

A Father's Words:

David was overwhelmed trying to choose a college and career. One night, his dad said, *"You don't have to figure everything out right now. God's not in a rush."* That conversation gave David room to breathe.

Try This:

- Share your own stories of uncertainty. Don't be afraid to let him see that you've wrestled, too.

- Sometimes, silence is more powerful than a speech. Just be there.

- Be willing to walk with him—even when the path winds in a direction you didn't expect.

When He Messes Up

At some point, your son will fall. He'll mess up, say the wrong thing, fail the test, disappoint someone—including himself. And in that moment, he needs you more than ever.

The Jesus Way:
Peter denied Jesus at his most vulnerable moment. Jesus didn't shame him—He restored him. That's the kind of grace your son needs at his lowest.

A Dad's Choice:
When Alex failed a major exam, he expected a lecture. Instead, his dad said, *"This doesn't define you."* That simple sentence gave Alex the courage to try again.

Try This:
- Choose grace before correction.
- Talk about what he can learn from the setback—but don't make it a lesson in shame.
- Celebrate effort and courage, not just achievements.

Looking to the Future Without Fear
The future can feel like a heavy burden for you and your son. Decisions about college, career, relationships—it's a lot. But God isn't overwhelmed by it. He's already there.

A Quiet Strength:
Liam was consumed with worry about the future. His dad didn't offer a five-point plan. He said, *"I don't know how it'll all turn out, but I believe God's got you."* That calm confidence helped Liam carry the weight differently.

Try This:
- Tell stories—how God showed up in your life, even when things didn't make sense at the time.
- Speak purpose over your son. Remind him of his strengths and of God's presence.
- Stay steady. Your peace becomes his anchor.

Prayer: The Lifeline

There will be days when you don't know what else to do—but you can always pray. Not perfectly. Just honestly.

Small Ways to Weave in Prayer:
- Whispering a prayer as he walks out the door.
- Ask, "Can we pray about that?" when life feels heavy.
- Keep a journal of prayers for him—it may mean the world someday.

Letting Go Isn't Letting Down

Letting go doesn't mean you stop caring—it means you start trusting. Trust that even in the mess, God's doing something good. Even in the detours, He's still leading.

Let your son wrestle, make mistakes, feel the weight of his own decisions, and remind him he doesn't carry that weight alone.

Building a Legacy That Lasts

You won't get it all right—no parent does. But what your son will remember most will not be the big talks or grand gestures—it will be your faith, your presence, and your patience.

Try This:

- Make small spiritual rhythms part of your home life—Sunday mornings, shared devotionals, or even short chats about God during car rides.

- Serve together—let him see your faith in action.

- Ask questions. Be willing to sit in the "I don't know" together.

Stories That Stick

- **Joseph**, Jesus' earthly father, said yes to a life of sacrifice and unknowns. Because of his quiet obedience, Jesus had a foundation of love and strength.

- **David**, a modern dad, watched his sons drift from faith. He didn't force them back—he invited them into connection. It was slow, but it worked.

- **The Bible describes Eli neglecting** to guide his sons. That warning still stands: presence and boundaries matter.

- **Mark** chased career success and missed the signs his son was struggling—until a crisis woke him up. He learned that your presence matters more than your paycheck.

Reflection

You don't need to be perfect. Just present. Faithful. Real.

You're not just raising a boy. You're raising a man of God. That's sacred ground—even when it's messy.

God is in this with you. On the hard days. In the beautiful moments. In the long, quiet stretches when you wonder if anything is sinking in.

Trust Him with your son's future—because He's the One writing the story.

Reflection Questions

1. What part of letting go feels hardest for you right now?
2. Are there expectations you need to release to God?
3. How can you make prayer more natural in your daily life?
4. How can you be more emotionally present this week?
5. What does building a faith legacy look like for your family?

Prayer for the Journey

"God, help me let go of control and hold on to trust.

Help me love my son with grace, not pressure.

Give me the wisdom to walk with him, not ahead of him.

And remind me, over and over, that you are writing a good story—even when I can't see the ending yet.

Amen."

Chapter 13:
Fatherhood That Leaves a Legacy: 11 Real-Life Lessons from the Frontlines

Father's Teaching #1: Seeking God's Face Through the Journey of Wisdom

The Beginning of the Journey

Ryan was a typical 15-year-old in many ways—full of curiosity and energy, always thinking, always questioning. School came easy to him. The equations? Simple. The essays? A breeze. Teachers loved him for his ability to grasp complicated ideas effortlessly. Yet, despite his academic success, a restless feeling was gnawing at him. A sense that something—something profound—was missing. No matter how many books he read or the problems he solved, life didn't add up.

It was on a late afternoon when Ryan sat at the kitchen table, staring at his homework but barely able to focus. The math problems in front of him felt empty, like hollow shells, devoid of meaning, which was not him.

"Dad," he said, his voice was quiet but carrying a sense of urgency, "I get all this stuff—math, history, science—but it feels... meaningless. I'm so tired of just learning for the sake of learning. There's gotta be something more to this, right? I want to know about my future and career, but how do I figure that out?"

Ryan's father, Caleb, had seen this look before—confusion and quiet desperation. He set down his coffee mug, his eyes soft but knowing. He'd walked this path and understood that Ryan wasn't just struggling with school. His son was wrestling with bigger questions: *What's the point? What's my purpose?*

"Son," Caleb said, leaning back slightly in his chair, "you're smart. You've got all the textbook knowledge you need. But there's something more important than just knowledge. You need wisdom—and that comes from seeking God's face."

Ryan looked at his father, the phrase *seeking God's face* hanging in the air, unfamiliar yet intriguing. "What do you mean? How does that help me with life's challenges? With figuring out what I should do, or how to make money?"

Caleb smiled gently. "It's not just about asking God for things. It's about asking for understanding—about your life, choices, and purpose. It's about building a relationship with God. When you connect with Him like that, you see the bigger picture. He helps you see clearly when everything else feels blurry."

Ryan was very quiet for a moment, then sighed. "I just feel... lost."

"I get it," Caleb said softly, "but trust me, things will start making sense when you seek God's wisdom. It won't happen all at once. It's a journey."

A Turning Point
Weeks passed, but the questions kept swirling in Ryan's mind. It was no longer just about school grades or choosing a career path. After losing a close friend, Ryan's perspective shifted—everything around him felt unfamiliar and uncertain, as if the solid ground he once stood on had suddenly become fragile and unsteady.

The world felt cracked open, and things he once took for granted no longer felt secure. Questions began to weigh heavily on his mind: *Why am I here? What's the point of all this?*

As he tried to picture his future, his thoughts grew increasingly tangled. It felt like trying to complete a puzzle with missing pieces—each answer only leading to more uncertainty.

He felt lost in a storm of doubt and grief, searching for something steady to hold onto—but not quite sure where to find it.

One night, lying in bed staring at the ceiling, his mind raced through the usual worries: choosing the right GCSEs, getting into a good university, finding a job. But then, amidst the chaos of his thoughts, he remembered something his dad had said: *Focus on God. Ask Him, and He will answer.*

Ryan tried to pray, but his mind kept slipping. One moment, he was thinking about his future—and the next, his mind wandered off to food, video games, or whatever show he was into. It was very frustrating. He wanted to focus, but his thoughts kept drifting all over the space. Still, something deep inside kept nudging him, gently pulling him back to God, even if it was just for a moment. Over time, Ryan started to notice a change. The distractions didn't magically go away, but there was a quiet peace starting to take root in him—a kind of calm that hadn't been there before. As the days went by, Ryan noticed something. The distractions didn't disappear altogether, but a quiet peace settled inside him.

As the days went by, Ryan began to notice a change. The distractions didn't vanish completely, but a quiet peace started to settle within him. Slowly, he was learning to quiet his mind, to tune out the noise. Prayer became less about asking for things and more about *listening* to God. The answers didn't always come immediately, but when they did, they felt deeper, more real than anything he'd ever learned in school, he learnt things that he was never taught by inspiration.

A New Kind of Prayer
Months passed, and Ryan could feel a shift happening within him. He was no longer praying just to ask for help with his homework which he used to do or future plans. He prayed more deliberately

to *listen*. And when he did, he felt God was showing him clarity, purpose, and direction. It wasn't just about receiving answers anymore. It was about learning to hear, discern God's voice and understanding life in a way that textbooks never could.

One afternoon, Ryan practically burst through the door, his face lighting up with much excitement. With a big smile and eyes shining, he looked up at his dad and said, "Dad, something feels different when I pray now. It's like I'm really hearing God more—like I can feel Him moving in my heart. He's been showing me things, things that were always there, but I just couldn't see before."

Caleb looked at his son, his heart quietly swelling with pride. There was something beautiful in that moment—a sign of growth, of faith beginning to take root. For a while, no words were needed—just a deep, shared understanding between father and son on this journey together.

"That's because when you seek God's face, He lights up your spirit," Caleb said gently. "It's like He's lighting a candle in your heart." You see things more clearly, but your mind has to be open to it. Prayer isn't just about talking to God—it's about listening. It's about understanding His guidance and letting that light guide your path."

Ryan nodded, feeling lighter. For the first time, he truly understood what prayer was about: not just a list of requests but a conversation with God, where the answers were often already waiting when we called, and God also rewards the effort of prayer by showing things that were never asked.

The Process of Illumination

As Ryan's journey continued, he began to be deliberate to pray for more profound wisdom—not just for his future but for his life, choices, what God wants him to do and values. As he prayed, he found himself drawn to the Book of Proverbs. It wasn't just words on a page anymore. Ancient wisdom spoke directly to him clearly, shaping his thoughts, calming his fears, and guiding his decisions.

One quiet evening, as the dishes were drying and the day was winding down, Ryan sat beside his dad, a little more thoughtful than usual.

"Dad," he said softly, "I had this dream a while back... I was flying a real plane—up in the sky, just me, soaring. It felt so real. And when I woke up... I don't know, I just *knew* it was from God."

His dad, Caleb, turned toward him with a smile that said he was listening with his whole heart. There was no teasing, no brushing it off—just a moment of deep attention.

"Ryan," he said gently, "that's not just a dream. That could be a glimpse of something bigger. Sometimes, God does speak to us like that—through dreams, or moments that stir something deep in us. It doesn't always come with thunder or lightning... sometimes it comes like this: quiet, powerful, and personal."

He paused and put a hand on Ryan's shoulder.

"Stay open, son. Keep your eyes and heart wide open. If that dream planted something in you, don't ignore it. It might just be part of the story God is writing in you." God speaks to us in many ways—through Scripture, moments of quiet reflection, and even the things you dream about. And when He does, it's a gift. You have to protect that gift."

Ryan paused, thinking about his distractions—the TV shows he watched, the music he listened to. "But what about the stuff I consume? I've noticed that it bothers me. Could it be blocking me from hearing God clearly?"

Caleb's expression grew serious. "Exactly. You need to protect your mind, son. What you feed your soul truly matters. Think about it—God created a skull to protect your brain because of how vital it is. He gave us a ribcage to shield our lungs and our heart. And because the spinal cord is so sensitive, He surrounded it with a strong vertebral column. Every essential part of our body was designed with protection. Every part... except the heart. God left that one unguarded—not by mistake, but by design. Why? Because He wants *you* to guard it. He made *you* the security agent around your own heart. The Bible says, 'Out of the heart flow the issues of life.' That means the state of your heart determines the direction of your life—it's like the geographical boundary of your being. If you let in things that pull you away from God, it'll get harder and harder to hear His voice. So guard your heart, son. Protect it like the treasure it is."

The Light of Revelation

As the months passed, Ryan's spiritual growth continued to deepen. He wasn't just reading Scripture anymore—he was living it. One evening, Caleb opened the Bible to Ephesians 1:15 and began to explain it.

"Ryan," he said, "seeking God's face is about opening the eyes of your understanding. It's like when Moses went into the tent of meeting, and God's glory filled the space. That's where real revelation happens. When you're in tune with God, you will get to see your life differently. You will see the purpose He has for you, the calling He's placed on your life, and the power He's given you experientially."

Ryan leaned in his heart racing. "So, it's all about seeing what God has planned for me, right?"

"Exactly," Caleb replied. "When you see with God's eyes, you understand that your life is part of a much bigger picture. God has a plan for you—your purpose—and He'll reveal it when you continue seeking Him. But it all starts with understanding who He is and who you are in Him."

The Wisdom of the Lord

Ryan sat back, his mind racing with everything he'd learned. This wasn't just a phase for Ryan. It wasn't a spiritual high that came and went, or a quick fix for when life felt confusing. It was something deeper—something real.

This journey of seeking God wasn't about checking boxes or having all the right answers. It was about building a relationship—slowly, honestly, one conversation at a time. Some days it meant asking hard questions. Other days, it meant sitting in silence, just trying to listen. And over time, Ryan started to notice the difference.

God's voice wasn't always loud or clear like a booming announcement. Sometimes, it came in ways that weren't strictly logical or easy to explain—what we might call *non-cognitive* communication. It wasn't always something Ryan could put into neat words or fully understand with his mind. Sometimes, God spoke through feelings, subtle nudges in his heart, or an inner knowing that didn't come from thinking but from sensing and knowing's.

These quiet, non-cognitive moments might feel like a gentle peace in the middle of chaos, a deep sense of direction when the path seemed unclear, a surge of life bubbling or a soft challenge to see things differently. It was like God was speaking in a language beyond words or logic—softly, patiently nudging Ryan's heart and mind, quietly changing how he saw the world and the decisions he made.

This wasn't just a brief moment or a fleeting experience—it was a lifelong journey. Ryan learned that faith isn't only about having clear, cognitive understanding or firm answers. It's about learning to notice God's quiet, steady presence—even when it's soft —and trusting those small feelings and instincts to lead and shape his life one step at a time. It was about walking *with* Him—day by day, through every season, and letting that relationship change him from the inside out.

Ryan wasn't just a teenager anymore, flipping through textbooks and hoping the right answers would suddenly click. Something was shifting. Slowly, quietly, he was becoming a young man—one who had started to look beyond the surface, beyond what everyone else expected of him.

He began to seek and search something deeper... not just facts, but the *truth*. Not just direction, but to find his *purpose*. And in that searching, he found himself drawn to God—not in a loud or overly dramatic way, but in real moments of prayer, reflection, and stillness. He started talking to God more honestly, listening carefully, and noticing how those quiet moments were shaping him.

And somewhere along the way, without realizing it, Ryan began to understand life differently from God's perspective. It wasn't just about getting everything right—it was about walking closely with the One who already knew the way. The questions didn't disappear, but they didn't scare him like they used to.

He was becoming grounded. Steady. Purposeful and deliberate.

And for the first time in a long time, he didn't feel lost. He felt led.

For Fathers and Sons: A Call to Seek Wisdom

This isn't just a story-It's a call to action Fathers, your role goes beyond teaching your sons how to navigate the world. It's about guiding them toward something deeper—the kind of wisdom that only comes from truly seeking God. As you walk with them through that journey, you're not just helping them figure out their path in life or career. You're helping them discover the purpose God uniquely designed for them—something they'll only uncover when they start to explore, just like astronauts reaching into the vast unknown of space.

This isn't just about finding success—it's about finding meaning in the journey . And that journey begins with the first step: seeking God's face.

Father's Teaching #2: Resisting Laziness and Building Discipline

"Go to the ant, O sluggard; consider her ways, and be wise."
– Proverbs 6:6 (ESV)

The Struggle

Let's be honest: most teen boys would choose YouTube, gaming, sleeping in over chores, studying, or reading Scripture. The digital age hasn't just offered distraction—it's trained young minds to expect **comfort without cost**, **pleasure without patience**, and **results without responsibility**.

Laziness isn't just about inactivity—it's often a symptom of a lack of vision, purpose, or structure. As a Christian parent, your task is to teach your son that manhood and maturity are built on **discipline, not desire**.

Why This Matters

A lazy boy becomes a passive man—disconnected from God's calling and unable to carry the weight of responsibility that adulthood demands.

God created boys to work, create, build, lead, and serve. Work isn't a punishment—it's part of God's design. When we instil discipline, we're not just raising obedient sons. We're raising strong men who can lead their homes, serve the church, and honour Christ with their hands and hearts.

Step-by-Step: Building Discipline and Drive in Your Son

1. Create a Simple, God-Centered Routine

- Boys thrive with structure—even if they resist it at first.
- Start small:
    - Wake up at a set time (even on weekends).
    - Make the bed.
    - 5-minute morning prayer or devotional.
    - Set 1 goal for the day (schoolwork, cleaning, physical, spiritual).
- Discipline begins in daily habits, not big declarations.

"Great men aren't made in big moments—they're made in everyday choices."

2. Assign Real Responsibility

- Give him meaningful tasks—not just busy work.
    - Chores with the purpose (taking out the trash, mowing, cooking once a week).
    - Help him see how his work contributes to the household's well-being.
- Tie responsibility to **honour**, not just obedience.

- - "You're old enough to carry more. I trust you with this."
- If he's old enough, help him find part-time work or serve in ministry.

3. Link Work to God's Purpose
- Teach that work is worship:
- *"Whatever you do, work at it with all your heart, as working for the Lord..."* – Colossians 3:23
- Help him discover and develop his gifts:
  - Is he creative? Encourage projects, not just screen time.
  - Is he athletic? Set goals and connect discipline in training to life.
- Explain how excellence reflects God's image.

4. Challenge, Don't Criticize
- Correct laziness, but don't attack identity.
  - Instead of: "You're so lazy."
  - Say: "I see more in you than this. Let's talk about why this is happening."
- When he follows through, **he celebrates effort**, not just outcome.

- Create a culture where **hard work is** not only expected but also praised.

5. Model the Lifestyle You Want Him to Live
- Let your son see you work hard with joy.
  - Around the house.
  - At your job.
  - In your spiritual life.
- Share your battles with laziness or procrastination—and how you fight back.
- Pray together for strength and motivation, especially during discouragement or fatigue.

Real-Life Story: The Lazy Summer That Changed Everything

Ethan was 15 when his dad gave him a choice at the start of summer:

"You can sleep in and waste three months, or we can set a schedule that helps you grow as a man."

Ethan chose the structure—reluctantly. They made a plan:

- Morning devotions and workouts.
- Reading a leadership book weekly.
- Volunteering at church twice a week.

By the end of the summer, Ethan had more confidence and a deeper walk with God. He also started mentoring younger boys. He still loved video games, but they no longer mastered him.

Discussion Questions for Parents
1. Where am I modelling discipline well—and where am I making excuses?
2. What's one daily habit I can help my son build this week?
3. How can I show my son that work is part of his calling, not a punishment?

Prayer for the Journey
Father, thank You for calling my son to more than comfort. Help me to train him with love and wisdom. Give him a heart that desires to work, serve, and lead with diligence. Show him that discipline brings freedom and that his efforts matter to You. In Jesus' name, amen.

Father's Teaching #3: Managing Anger and Emotional Control

"Be angry and do not sin; do not let the sun go down on your anger." – **Ephesians 4:26 (ESV)**

The Struggle

Anger in teen boys is often misunderstood. It's not always rebellion. Sometimes it's fear. Sometimes it's pain. Sometimes, it's pressure they don't know how to process. But if left unchecked, that anger can erupt in outbursts, harm relationships, or turn inward as depression or bitterness.

As a Christian father, your role is not just to stop the explosion but to disciple your son toward emotional strength and godly self-control.

Why This Matters

Boys are often told, "Real men don't cry" or "toughen up." These cultural lies keep them from developing healthy emotional tools. But God's Word paints a different picture. Jesus showed righteous anger, deep compassion, and even wept. Teaching your son how to feel deeply and still choose wisdom is one of the most critical lessons for lifelong success and godly manhood.

Step-by-Step: Helping Your Son Control His Emotions Without Shutting Down

1. Normalize the Emotion, Not the Outburst
- Teach that anger is a natural emotion—what you do with it is what truly matters.
- Use real examples:
  - Jesus flipping tables in righteous anger (John 2:13–17).
  - David poured out frustration in Psalms—but still trusted God.
- Let your son know: "It's okay to feel, but feelings can't lead."

"Son, emotions are signals—not steering wheels."

2. Identify Emotional Triggers
- Help him notice patterns:
  - Does he get angry when he feels disrespected?
  - When he's tired, hungry, or overwhelmed?
- Use tools like:
  - A "Feelings Chart" to name emotions more accurately (e.g., frustrated vs. furious).
  - Journaling a few sentences daily: "Today I felt ___ when ___ happened."

- Encourage self-awareness over shame.

3. Teach the "Stop-Think-Pray" Method

A simple tool that works in the heat of the moment:

- **STOP** – Take a breath. Step away if needed.
- **THINK** – What am I feeling? Why? What are the consequences?
- **PRAY** – Ask God for help to respond with peace and wisdom.

Role-play scenarios together:

- "Someone cuts you off in traffic—what do you do?"
- "A friend mocks your faith—how do you respond?"

4. Model It in Real Life

- Your example matters more than your lecture.
- If you blow up, don't justify it—apologize. Say:
    - "I got angry. I was wrong. Will you forgive me?"
    - "Let's both keep growing in this area."
- This teaches your son the importance of humility and how to take responsibility.

"We don't need perfect dads. We need present and honest ones."

5. Create a Grace-Filled Environment

- Make your home a safe place for emotional expression, not a war zone.

- When your son feels out of control, respond with calm strength—not shouting.

- Build family habits of peace:

    - End the day with prayer.

    - Speak blessings over one another.

    - Practice forgiveness quickly.

Real-Life Story: The Explosion That Changed Everything

Sam, a 14-year-old from a Christian home, had a short fuse. One night, after being told to put down his phone, he threw it across the room and screamed, "I hate this house!"

His father's response? He walked over, sat beside him, and said calmly, "That wasn't okay—but I can see you're carrying something heavy. What's going on?"

Sam broke down. Behind the anger was anxiety over school, social media, and not feeling good enough.

That conversation didn't just calm the moment—it opened the door to more profound healing. His dad began regular one-on-one time with him, and today, Sam journals his emotions and leads a small group of younger boys at church.

Discussion Questions for Parents

1. How do I respond when my son gets angry—do I escalate or de-escalate the situation?

2. Have I taught him that emotions are part of God's design, not signs of weakness?

3. What practical steps can we take this week to help him build emotional awareness?

Prayer for the Journey

Father, help me guide my son through his emotions with wisdom, understanding and grace. Teach him that anger is not his master but that Your Spirit brings self-control and peace. Help us both reflect Jesus—even when our feelings are loud. In Jesus' name, amen.

Father's Teaching #4 – The Secret of Greatness: Tending the Gift

It was one of those slow, golden Saturday mornings—the kind where the world feels unhurried, like even time is taking a breath. The breeze rolled gently through the trees, and the porch creaked under the weight of two people simply being present.

Michael sat next to his father, both nursing mugs of warm cocoa. Their hands were still dirty from the garden, but neither seemed in a rush to wash up. The silence between them wasn't awkward; it was shared, understood—like a song without words.

His father looked over at him. Studied him.

Michael was growing—not just taller, but deeper. The wide-eyed questions about dinosaurs and galaxies had quieted into thoughtful pauses and long, slow stares into the sky. Something was shifting. The boy was turning into a man.

His father spoke quietly.

Father:
"Mike, I've been watching you. You've got something inside—a gift. You've always had it. I see it when you talk about music, when you get caught up in an idea, and your whole face lights up. That spark? That's from God."

Michael gave a little shrug, staring into his cup.

Michael:

"I don't know, Dad... I'm just messing around with music. Doesn't feel like much of a gift."

Father:

"Most gifts don't at first. They start small—like seeds. But here's the thing: even a seed that can grow into a towering oak still needs tending. A gift left alone doesn't become greatness. It becomes... potential. That's not what you were made for."

He paused, letting it settle.

Father (continued):

"There was a young man I knew. Talented, like you. But he learned early that the real engine behind his gift wasn't just practice—it was prayer. He fasted once a week. Not for attention, not for points—but to stay close to God. He realized something: a gift without God is just noise."

Michael looked up.

Michael:

"Did it work? Like... did it matter?"

Father:

"It changed everything. See, Mark 3:14 says Jesus appointed the twelve *that they might be with Him,* and *then* that He might send them out. That's the order. Be with Him first—*then* you're sent. That young man found out that when he moved without God, things were hit or miss. But when he waited, when he stayed close—there was power in his presence. Authority."

He leaned forward a little.

Father:
"Imagine someone stands in traffic and tries to stop cars. No one listens. But if that same person puts on a police uniform? Every car halts. Why? Authority. That's what it means to be *sent*. It's not about volume—it's about who's backing you. God in the midst. Your gift, when tended in God's presence, gets backed by heaven. And that changes *everything*."

Michael's eyes narrowed thoughtfully.

Michael:
"So the power isn't just in talent—it's in the source."

Father:
"Exactly. There's a difference between performing and carrying presence. That young man built a secret history with God—through prayer and quiet moments that nobody saw. And when he sang, people didn't just clap—they cried. Prayed. Changed. One woman told his mother, 'I haven't stopped praying since he sang.' That's not talent. That's fire from the altar."

Michael exhaled. The silence between them stretched, weighty.

Michael:

"That's... heavy."

Father:

"It is. Greatness always costs something. But in God's Kingdom, the path up always starts down—in hiddenness, in humility. That's where the fire is tended."

He looked Michael straight in the eyes.

Father:

"Isaiah 60:3 says, *'Nations will come to your light, and kings to the brightness of your rising.'* You know what that means? Even when your gift is just a spark, hungry people will notice. But when you grow it—when it burns bright—it doesn't just draw the hungry. It draws kings. People of influence. Leaders. The weighty ones. You weren't made just to reach wanderers, Mike. You were made to move nations. But that requires fire. Not flickers."

Michael sat still, his chest rising a little deeper now.

Michael:

"So... don't settle for being seen. Be sent."

Father:

"That's it. Don't chase applause when you're called to carry presence. When the presence of God is with a man, His power is with him. Don't stay in the outer courts when you're invited into the throne room. Tend your gift. Sharpen it in secret. Stay close to

Him—because it's not about being seen, it's about being sent. And when the time comes, watch what God does."

Father's Teaching #5 – Building the Altar (Featuring Alta)

The porch still held its calm—birds chirping in the trees, sunlight resting gently on the railings—but something in Michael had changed. He wasn't just sitting anymore; he was leaning forward, elbows on his knees like the weight of a question had settled into his bones. His eyes weren't just curious—they were searching. It was like something had broken open inside him—gently but deeply. Not just interest anymore... hunger. A quiet ache rose in his chest. For something real. Something he couldn't quite explain but sincerely, desperately wanted to find.

Michael looked up, his voice almost a whisper.

Michael:
"Okay... but how do I start? I mean, really start. How do you *actually* hear God like that?" His voice was filled with quiet anticipation, a hunger for something he couldn't quite explain but desperately wanted to find.

His father, a man of deep faith and wisdom, didn't answer right away. He just looked at him—eyes kind, a little misty. The kind of look people have when they're about to hand over something sacred, like a secret that's been guarded for generations.

He smiled. Slow. Soft. His calm demeanour is a soothing balm to Michael's restless soul.

Like he knew exactly what this moment meant to Michael.

Father:

"You start by building your altar."

He tapped his chest with two fingers.

Father (contd):

"Right here. It doesn't begin with lights or microphones. It starts in the quiet. Five honest minutes a day. Just you and God. That's your altar. That's where the conversation begins."

Michael:

"Five minutes? That's all?"

Father:

His father did smiled—gently, the kind of smile that said I've been there too. The type of smile that spoke more than words ever could. There was a quiet understanding in his eyes, the kind that made Michael feel safe and seen.

Father:

"Five minutes… when it's real?"

He paused, letting the weight of it settle.

"That's everything."

His voice was low, steady—like truth wrapped in warmth.

Father:

"It is not about staring at a clock. It's about who shows up. God's not counting minutes, Michael. He's watching the heart. And when your heart is open—even for just five honest minutes—He'll be there. Every time."

Michael exhaled softly, like something tight inside him had just been released. He's watching your heart."

He leaned back slowly, letting the silence do some of the talking.

Then, softer:

"An altar, Michael... It's not just a wooden table in a church. It's the space you carve out—right in the middle of your ordinary life. A corner of your room. A moment in your day. It's where heaven finds you. But here's the part most people miss: it doesn't start up there," he nodded gently toward the sky. "It starts down here. With you. With a whisper. A prayer. An invitation."

He leaned in, voice dropping low.

Father (contd):

"Matthew 18:18 says, 'Whatever you bind on earth will be bound in heaven… whatever you loose on earth will be loosed in heaven.' *Earth initiates.* Heaven responds. That's how God set it up. That's why prayer isn't just devotion—it's permission." His words carried a weight of wisdom that enlightened Michael.

Michael blinked, caught by the weight of it.

Michael:

"You mean... God *waits* for us to invite Him?"

Father:

"Yes. Just like you need a visa to enter another country—heaven doesn't just barge in. The altar is your embassy. It's how you give God legal access to move in your life. If there's no altar, there's no invitation. No permission."

He paused, letting the truth of it breathe.

Father:

"God is a King—and a gentleman. He keeps to His own protocol. He waited for Adam. Called out, 'Where are you?' But Satan? He doesn't wait. He doesn't ask. He found Eve and disregarded God's protocol."

Michael's hands gripped the sides of his mug now, the cocoa inside long forgotten.

Father:

"That's why we build it. Because without an altar, the wrong presence enters. But when there *is* an altar—when someone on earth says, 'God, I welcome You here'—everything changes."

He pulled out a folded note from his back pocket. Creased and worn.

Father:

"Anita wrote this when she was first learning to hear Him. She said, 'The altar isn't a stage. It's not a platform. It's a door.' That girl—we watched her build her altar through poetry, journaling, nights of tears and silence. And every time—*He came.*"

Michael read the words on the note—his sister's messy, passionate handwriting—and held them like a treasure.

Father:

"Your altar might be different. It might look like music. Or five quiet minutes in your room. Doesn't matter. What matters is that you build it. Consistently. Faithfully. That you show up."

Michael's voice was quiet now.

Michael:

"What if I mess it up?"

His father chuckled gently.

Father:

"You will. We all do. But God doesn't need perfect—He needs honesty. The altar isn't just a beginning—it's a *return point*. The strongest people aren't the ones who never stumble. They're the ones who know how to come back. Fast."

He placed a firm hand on Michael's shoulder.

Father:
"Don't ignore the Holy Spirit, son. He's gentle... not loud or pushy. If you push Him away, He won't storm out—but He also won't barge back in. He waits. Quietly. Lovingly. But if you just turn—just whisper, *'I'm sorry... come close again'*—He always does. No hesitation. That's the kind of God He is."

He reached over, gently placing a hand on Michael's shoulder.

Father (softly):
"Stay tender. Stay soft. That's how you keep the fire burning. Pride puts it out. But humility? Humility keeps the flame alive."

Michael nodded slowly. Eyes lowered. Then, after a moment, he looked up and asked quietly:

Michael:
"...But what if I mess up again?"

Michael:
"But... how do I *know* He's with me?"

His father smiled. But there was a fire in his eyes now.

Father:
"Because He shows up. Just like He did for Joshua. Do you remember Jericho? Everyone saw walls. But Joshua—he saw a warrior. Sword drawn. An officer of heaven's army."

He paused, voice rising with quiet awe.

Father (contd):

"God opened his eyes to see that the army of Israel wasn't humans fighting alone. Angels had been sent—*on assignment*. Divine soldiers, synchronized with human footsteps. Marching as one. And that warrior didn't say, 'I'm on your side.' He said, 'I take orders from God.' Joshua thought he was in command... but heaven had already been deployed."

Michael's breath caught—sharp, quiet.

Something clicked deep inside, like puzzle pieces sliding into place—pieces he hadn't even known he was holding.

His chest rose slowly, eyes blinking, almost as if seeing everything with new clarity. The story of Joshua, the altar, the presence—it wasn't just history anymore. It was an invitation. Real. Immediate.

He looked at his father, voice hushed, awed:

Michael:

"All this time... I thought it was just strategy. Just bravery. But Joshua—he wasn't fighting alone."

His father nodded, the kind of nod that carried weight—truth felt, not just known.

Michael:

"So, Joshua wasn't just leading men?" His voice was barely above a whisper. "He was leading with heaven?"

His eyes searched his father's face, wide with the weight of it—not just awe, but a realization. Like he'd just glimpsed how much more there was to the battles he might one day face.

His father nodded slowly, like a confirmation and a commissioning all at once.

Father:
"Exactly."

He leaned in a little, voice hushed like he was letting Michael in on a sacred secret.

"That's what an altar does—it brings you into heaven's rhythm. It lines your heart up with something bigger... something eternal."

He paused, eyes searching Michael's face.

Father:
"The help you need? It's not always going to come from people. Sometimes, it's invisible. But that doesn't make it any less real. It's supernatural. Angels. Wisdom. Strength you didn't know you had. But here's the thing—"

His voice dropped a note, serious now.

"It won't come unless you call for it."

Michael sat back slowly, something burning quietly behind his ribs. A fire—not loud, not wild—but steady. Alive. Like a new hunger had just been named.

Father:

"Amos 9:1 says, 'I saw the Lord standing at the altar.' He didn't send an angel. He *came*. When you build your altar, God doesn't outsource. He invades. Personally. The secret of the church has never been their preaching—it's *the presence*."

His voice dropped to a whisper.

Father:

"The devil will do everything to keep you from praying. He'll distract you with things that feel good but drain life. That's because he knows—your altar is dangerous. It's how you open the door."

Michael's voice was quiet. Steady.

Michael:

"I want that. Not just the knowledge. I want direction. Presence. Power." (This is why Daniel prayed three times a day and every day to gain access to secrets and divine intelligence)

Father:

"Then start. Today. Five to 10 minutes. Music, stillness, a whisper—just make space. Say, 'Holy Spirit, I'm here. You're welcome here.' Let Him teach you. Let Him speak. That's the technology of the altar—it keeps you connected. Intimate. Aligned."

Michael stood something locked in place within him.

Michael:

"Alright. I'll do it. Five minutes. I'll build my altar."

His father smiled and placed his hand over Michael's heart.

Father:

"Good. Let's build it together—starting now. Because son... the strongest man isn't the smartest. It's the one who's closest to the Holy Spirit."

Father's Teaching #6: Navigating Doubt and Building Real Faith

"Train up a child in the way he should go; even when he is old he will not depart from it." – Proverbs 22:6 (ESV)

The Struggle

Many Christian teenage boys attend **church but do not grow in their faith in Christ**. They know the correct answers in Sunday school, but inside, they're wrestling with questions they're afraid to ask:

- "Is God really real?"
- "Why do bad things happen?"
- "Does faith even make a difference?"

In today's culture—where deconstruction and doubt are common—if a teen doesn't **own his faith**, he will likely leave it behind.

As a parent, your goal is not to force belief but to **walk beside your son as he discovers** what it means to follow Jesus for himself.

Why This Matters

Faith can't just be taught—it must be **caught** and **confirmed** through genuine encounters with God. And those encounters often begin with tough questions, doubts, and seasons of wrestling.

It's not your job to be His Holy Spirit—but your calling is to cultivate an environment where faith can grow strong roots.

Step-by-Step: Leading Your Son to Personal, Rooted Faith

1. Invite His Doubts—Don't Dismiss Them

- When your son asks, "How do we even know the Bible is true?" don't panic.

- Respond with curiosity, not correction:
    - "That's a great question. Let's explore it together."

- Say "I don't know" when needed—but always follow up with a plan to dig deeper together.

"Doubt isn't the enemy of faith. Silence and shame are."

2. Help Him Develop a Personal Relationship with Jesus

- Don't just say, "Read your Bible." *Model it. Do it with him.*

- Start with short, relevant reading plans (Proverbs, Luke, or James).

- Encourage journaling:
    - What is God saying to me?
    - What do I need help trusting Him with?

- Challenge him to pray out loud—even if it's just one sentence.

3. Expose Him to Real Faith in Action

- Take him to youth camps and mission trips, or serve together at church.
- Let him see faith lived in real-life stories:
  - Invite mentors, leaders, or older guys who love Jesus into his world.
  - Watch testimonies or movies that stir spiritual hunger.

Faith grows best in the soil of relationships and real-life experiences.

4. Encourage Ownership of Spiritual Habits

- Let him choose his Bible translation, journal style, or devotional book.
- Teach him to give from his allowance or first paycheck.
- Let him help lead family prayer or pick worship songs.
- Encourage him to ask God what *he* wants to do—not just what you expect.

5. Be a Safe Place When His Faith Wavers

- Stay close if he messes up, backslides, or walks through spiritual dryness.

- Remind him that God's love doesn't depend on performance:
    - "God's grace doesn't run out when you're struggling."
    - "Let's walk through this together."
- Keep praying for him, even when he pulls away, which mostly happens.

Real-Life Story: The Question That Changed Everything

Isaiah was 17, a church kid through and through. One night, he told his dad, "I don't know if I believe in this. What if we're wrong?"

His dad didn't get defensive. Instead, he said:

"I've had doubts too. Let's take the next few weeks and explore your questions. No judgment."

They began meeting once a week—reading Scripture, listening to apologetics podcasts, and asking hard questions together. Six months later, Isaiah chose to get baptized again—not to please his dad, but because he genuinely believed.

Discussion Questions for Parents

1. How do I respond when my son expresses doubt—do I shut it down or open a door?
2. Is my own faith visible, active, and alive—or only theoretical?

3. What spiritual experiences or mentors can I help connect my son to this year?

Prayer for the Journey

Lord, I surrender my son's heart to You. Help me guide him with truth, humility, and grace. Strengthen his faith—not just as knowledge but as a relationship. Use me and others to reveal Your love and presence in real ways. Draw him near, even through his doubts. In Jesus' name, amen.

Father's Teaching #7: The Voice of God vs. The Voice of Man

Theme: *Guiding Sons Through Rebellion with Grace, Boundaries, and the Voice of God*

Setting the Scene: A Conversation Between Generations

It was a warm Sunday afternoon. The garden buzzed quietly with birdsong, and the scent of jasmine drifted in on a lazy breeze. James, silver-haired and steady in his early sixties, sat across from his son, Michael, on the weathered patio chairs. A steaming mug of tea warmed James's hands as he studied the lines of tension carved into Michael's face.

James:

"Michael, you look like you've been carrying the world on your shoulders. Raising a teenager—especially one who's starting to push back—cuts deeper than most people realize, doesn't it?"

Michael sighed, rubbing a hand through his short, dark hair.

Michael:

"I'm trying, Dad. I am. I lay down rules because I want to keep him safe and steer him in the right direction. But the harder I try, the more distant he gets. Says I don't get him. He says I'm too religious, too stuck in the past. And the thing is... maybe he's right. I don't even know if what I'm doing is helping anymore."

James nodded slowly, his eyes holding a quiet understanding. There was no rush to speak at the time—just the kind of look that said, *I've been there too.*

James:
"Sounds familiar. You might not remember, but there were days you made me feel the same way. I thought I was out of touch, too strict. Truth is, the distance isn't always a rejection—it's them trying to find their feet. But they still need to feel you're there. Steady. Listening, even when they're not talking."

Michael looked down at his hands for a moment, then back up.

Michael:
"Feels like I'm fumbling through this blind."

James offered a faint smile.

James:
"You are. We all did. But loving them through the confusion—that's what they'll remember."

James:
"I've been there, son. Adding more rules would build a better fence around sin. But then I learned something—something from Genesis, of all places..."

And so, he began to tell the story of Adam and Eve and the subtle danger of adding man's voice to God's.

STEP 1: Shift Your Mindset – See Rebellion as an Opportunity

Biblical Principle: *"The wise in heart are called discerning, and gracious words promote instruction."* – Proverbs 16:21

James (continued):

"Remember how God told Adam not to eat from the tree? That was the rule—simple and clear. But when Eve talks to the serpent, she adds, 'We must not even touch it.' That wasn't God's voice. That was Adam's addition. A rule made out of fear."

Michael:

"So even though it was meant to protect, it backfired?"

James:

"Exactly. She touched the fruit, and when nothing happened, she began to question the truth of the command itself. That's the danger of parenting from fear."

Just like Caleb and his son Jonah...

Story: Jonah's Withdrawal

Jonah, fifteen, had stopped talking to his dad, Caleb. Their once easy conversations had turned into slammed doors and silence. Caleb felt like shutting everything down—cutting off phones, cancelling outings, just giving up. But then he reminded himself of something important: every conflict was a chance to guide Jonah toward what mattered.

So, instead of punishing them, Caleb invited Jonah to breakfast one morning. Over pancakes and coffee, Jonah finally opened up. He admitted to feeling anxious as the pressure school was building up, and he didn't know how to handle it.

Tip:

- When your child's acting out, try to pause and ask yourself: *What is my child's heart trying to say?* Sometimes, the behaviour is just the surface of something more profound.

- Use conflict as a connection, not condemnation.

STEP 2: Set Clear, Loving Boundaries

Biblical Principle: *"Let your 'Yes' be 'Yes,' and your 'No,' be 'No'; anything beyond this comes from the evil one." – Matthew 5:37*

Michael (reflecting):

"I told my son he's not allowed on social media at all. I said, 'God doesn't want you wasting time with foolish things.' But now... I'm wondering if I made it sound like God said something He didn't."

James:

"That's what I did with you and that youth concert. I said 'no' out of fear, not faith. I didn't teach—I just restricted. And it drove a wedge between us."

Like Sarah with her son Daniel...

Story: Daniel and the Curfew

After Daniel broke curfew several times, his mom, Sarah, changed her approach. She didn't raise her voice. No threats, no dramatic punishments. Just a calm, steady tone.

"If you're late, you lose the car for a week. "That's what trust is," she said gently. "You take care of it. If it breaks, you don't just get it back—you work to rebuild it."

She wasn't trying to control him. She just wanted to be clear. Daniel needed to know where the lines were—not to trap him, but to give him something solid to stand on. It wasn't about catching him out. It was about helping him see the weight of his choices and giving him space to step up.

At first, he pushed back—rolled his eyes, muttered under his breath. But over time, something shifted. He started checking in. Being on time. Not because he was scared but because understanding kicked in, to know that trust wasn't automatic. It had to be built—and protected.

Tip:

Be clear about expectations and consequences—and always explain the reasons behind them so that it is well understood. Boundaries aren't about control; they're about building trust.

Step 3: Begin Early – Lay the Foundation Before the Storm

Biblical Principle: "Train up a child in the way he should go; even when he is old he will not depart from it." — Proverbs 22:6

James leaned back in his chair, his voice soft but firm.

James:

"David didn't raise Solomon with fear. He prepared him for leadership. He reminded him to walk with God (1 Chronicles 22). That's the kind of father you want to be. Not reactive—intentional."

Like Rachel and her son Micah...

Story: Prepping Before the Storm

When Micah was 13, Rachel started "Coffee & Christ" mornings—reading Scripture and praying before school. By 16, when temptations and peer pressure mounted, Micah came to her first—not last.

Actionable Tip:

- Don't wait for the crisis. Plant gospel seeds early.
- Build a rhythm of openness that makes later conversations natural.

Faith Over Fear: Two Voices, Two Outcomes

James:

"The Pharisees added rule upon rule and missed the heart of God. But Jesus? He met people where they were. He spoke truth with grace. That's our model."

Practical Tools to Apply

Common Concern: *"Am I too strict or too lenient?"*

- Reflect: Is this rule based on fear or faith?
- Let grace and truth walk hand in hand.

Common Concern: *"How do I rebuild trust?"*

- Be honest: "I didn't handle that right. Will you forgive me?"
- Humility heals faster than harshness.

Discussion Prompts for Parents

- What rules have I made that God didn't command?
- Where have I corrected behaviour without connecting to the heart?
- When was the last time I apologized to my child?

Reflection Questions for Journaling

- What parts of my parenting come from fear, not Scripture?

- What story is my son writing in his heart because of how I respond?

- How can I turn down my voice and turn up God's?

Encouragement: Lead from God's Heart, Not Man's Habits

Parenting today is loud and overwhelming. However, do not let fear weaken you. The most audible voice your child hears should be one of faith, not fear. Your job isn't to be perfect—it's to be present. To be honest. To reflect God's love and truth more than your traditions.

Let God's voice shape your rules, your tone, and your love.

The teenage years don't have to be a battleground.

They can become a **beautiful bridge**—if you walk it together, hand in hand with Christ.

Father's Teaching #8: Handling Peer Pressure and Identity Crises

"Do not conform to the pattern of this world, but be transformed by the renewing of your mind."
– **Romans 12:2 (NIV)**

The Struggle

Teen boys today are navigating an identity battlefield unlike any generation before. Social media, culture wars, digital influencers, and peer groups preach loud messages about who they should be: tough, popular, sexual, and "Cool." But few voices are helping them ask, "Who does God say I am?"

At the same time, the fear of peer rejection or exclusion can lead even grounded boys to compromise their values.

Your role as a father is to plant your identity deep enough that no storm—peer pressure, doubt, or culture—can uproot it.

Why This Matters

A boy who doesn't know who he is will become whatever the crowd demands. But a boy who understands his identity in Christ can stand even when he stands alone.

Identity shapes everything—his choices, confidence, relationships, and even how he views God. Peer pressure isn't just a temptation problem—it's an identity problem.

Step-by-Step: Helping Your Son Build Unshakable Identity

1. Affirm His Identity in Christ—Often

Speak life over him regularly: *"You are chosen. You are called. You are deeply loved by God."*

- Use Scriptures like:
    - **1 Peter 2:9** – "You are a royal priesthood..."
    - **Galatians 2:20** – "Christ lives in me..."
    - **Ephesians 2:10** – "You are God's workmanship..."
- **Tip:** Write affirmations on his mirror, notebook, or phone background.

"The loudest voice he hears should be yours, reminding him of God's truth."

Why? Because your words have the power to change things, to shape your child's reality.

Acts 10:44 says, *"While Peter was still speaking, the Holy Ghost fell..."*—that's the power of spoken words. As Peter released the word, the Spirit moved. Not after. Not before. *While* he was saying. This immediate impact is what makes your role so crucial.

Now, imagine this: You're in a room, and someone passes gas. The foul odour spreads quickly—it takes over the atmosphere. That's what it's like when the world speaks death, fear, and negativity—it fills the space. But the moment you spray a beautiful perfume, that foul smell is overtaken. The sweet fragrance lingers. Speaking is like that. When you talk about life—God's Word, truth, identity—you shift the atmosphere. You replace fear with faith.

Jesus said, *"The words I speak to you are spirit and life."* So when you speak, you're not just making sound—you're releasing Spirit and life into the room, into your child, into the moment.

Here's another example: If I ask you to count from 1 to 10 in your mind—go ahead, start... Now, say the word *"Great"* out loud. What happened? You stopped counting. Why? Because **speaking overrides thinking**. The moment you spoke, your brain had to pause the internal thought to respond to the voice. That's what happens when you talk about life—it interrupts the lies, silences the noise, and overrides the enemy's whispers.

This is why we must constantly affirm our children's identity in Christ with our words. It's not enough to hope they know—**tell them**. Over and over, with persistence and dedication.

"You are chosen.

You are called.

You are set apart.

You are loved."

Let your voice be louder than the world's noise. Speak—because that's how heaven touches earth.

2. Prepare Him for the pressure

- **Role-play scenarios**: "What would you do if your friends started vaping?"

- Teach the power of a firm "no" and the freedom to walk away.

- Share your own past peer pressure stories—wins and failures.

- Help him create **pre-decisions**: "When this happens, I already know what I'll do."

3. Surround Him with Godly Community

- **Action**: Get him involved in a Christ-centered youth group or mentorship.

- Invite strong male role models into his life (uncles, coaches, church leaders).

- Let your home be where his friends are welcome—*you* be the influence.

"You become like the people you hang out with. Let's make sure those people are building you up."

4. Give Him a Purpose Bigger Than Popularity

- Help him identify gifts and talents—and encourage him to use them for God's glory.

    o Music? Encourage worship or production.

    o Sports? Talk about leadership and sportsmanship as a ministry.

    o Technology? Challenge him to build, create, or mentor others.

- A young man with vision is less likely to chase approval.

5. Stay Close—Even When He Pushes Away

- He may act like he doesn't need you—but he does.

- Create small moments of connection: Drive-time chats, late-night snacks, and weekly check-ins.

- Ask open-ended questions:

    o "What was the best part of your day?"

    o "Anything confusing or challenging going on at school?"

Presence, not perfection, makes the difference.

Real-Life Story: A Son's "Cool" Nearly Cost Him

Marcus was 16 when his group of friends started shoplifting for thrills. At first, he watched, then joined in.

When the school called his dad, Marcus was expecting rage. Instead, his dad calmly asked, "Why did you feel like you had to be one of them?"

"I don't know," Marcus said. "I just didn't want to be the weird one."

His father responded, "Son, being different is a blessing. You don't need to fit in—you're set apart."

That day marked the beginning of a year-long journey to restore Marcus' sense of worth—not in friends, but in God. Today, Marcus mentors middle schoolers in his church's youth group.

Discussion Questions for Parents

1. What messages is my son receiving about who he should be—from school, media, or friends?
2. How can I practically affirm his identity in Christ this week?
3. Is he surrounded by a community that pushes him toward God or away?

Prayer for the Journey

Lord, help me speak life into my son. Let him know that his worth is found not in the crowd but in Christ. Strengthen him to stand firm when pressured, and remind him he is never alone. Give me wisdom to guide him with grace and truth. In Jesus' name, amen.

Father's Teaching #9: Overcoming Pornography and Lust

"I will set no worthless thing before my eyes; I hate the work of those who fall away; it shall not cling to me."
– Psalm 101:3 (ESV)

The Struggle

You don't need statistics to know that pornography is one of the most pervasive challenges teen boys face today. It's accessible 24/7, often introduced as early as 9 or 10, shaping how our sons view their bodies, women, relationships, and faith.

As Christian fathers and parents, our goal is not just to stop the behaviour but to disciple the heart—to raise sons who pursue holiness, respect women, and learn how to fight temptation with truth and accountability.

Why This Matters

Pornography doesn't just affect behaviour—it rewires the brain, distorts identity, and hardens the heart toward God's design for sexuality. It creates secrecy and shame, barriers to spiritual and emotional maturity. So that the love of God becomes cold.

When we teach purity, we protect our sons from harm and call them to something better: God's vision for manhood, integrity, and intimacy.

Step-by-Step: Helping Your Son Fight for Purity

1. Start Open Conversations (Not Interrogations)

- **Tip:** Ask, "What are kids at school saying about sex or porn?" rather than "Have you looked at porn?"

- Share your own past or present struggles in an age-appropriate way. Vulnerability creates safety.

- Set the tone: This is not about catching or shaming—it's about growth and trust.

*"Dad, I thought I'd be punished if I told you..." – **Teen Son***

*"I'm proud of you for being honest. Let's work through this together." – **Dad***

2. Set Boundaries and Use Accountability Tools

- **Action:** Install parental filters and accountability software, such as **Covenant Eyes** or **Bark**.

- Have clear rules: No phones are allowed behind closed doors, internet is not allowed after a specific time, and devices are always charged outside the bedroom.

- But remember: **Boundaries are not substitutes for discipleship.** They are tools, not the solution.

3. Teach God's Vision of Purity

- **Scripture study:** Read together Matthew 5:27–30. Let Jesus define the standard.
- What does honouring God with your eyes, thoughts, and body mean?
- Help him understand that purity isn't just abstinence—it's alignment with God's design for love, sex, and self-control.

4. When He Falls, Be a Father, Not a Judge

- Don't freak out if your son confesses to watching porn. Instead:
    - Thank him for telling you.
    - Ask what triggered it (boredom, stress, curiosity).
    - Work together to build better strategies.
- Reinforce grace: God's mercy is new every morning (Lamentations 3:23).

"You fell, but you're not a failure. Let's get back up and fight together."

5. Be a Living Example of Integrity

- Let him see that purity is something you care about, too.
- Share how you guard your own eyes, thoughts, and heart.
- Pray before him for strength, and invite him to do the same.

Real-Life Story: The Father Who Leaned In

Jason's 15-year-old son, Luke, cried one night after church. "Dad, I've been watching porn almost every day. I don't know how to stop. I hate myself."

Jason's first reaction was anger—but he paused, prayed, and looked his son in the eyes. "Thank you for telling me. That takes courage. This doesn't change how I see you. We're going to get through this."

Together, they:

- Set up accountability tools.
- Started reading Proverbs together each morning.
- Attended a father-son weekend on sexual purity.

A year later, Luke battles temptation but no longer fights alone and knows grace.

Discussion Questions for Parents

1. When was the last time you talked to your son about pornography or lust? Was it a conversation or a lecture?
2. What accountability tools can you put in place this week?
3. How can you model a life of purity and grace in your behaviour?

Prayer for the Journey

Father, give me the courage to speak the truth with love. Help my son see himself as You see him—clean, redeemed, and strong in You. Give us both the strength to fight temptation and walk in the light. In Jesus' name, amen.

Father's Teaching #10: A Father's Heart-to-Heart – Guiding Sons Through Sexuality

"Hey, bud. I've been noticing a few things lately—your voice is getting deeper, you've been a bit quieter than usual, and there's this look in your eyes like you've got a lot going on up there. Are you okay?" Son: "Yeah... I guess. It's just weird. I no longer feel like a little boy, but I don't exactly feel grown up either. It's like I'm stuck in between, trying to figure out who I am supposed to be." Father: "I do get that. And honestly? That's completely normal. You're not alone in that feeling. This stage—adolescence—is like standing at the edge of a bridge. One foot on what you have known, the other reaching for who you are becoming. Your body is changing, your mind is asking bigger questions, and your emotions are all over the place some days. That is not just normal; it's a sign that you're growing." (leans in, grinning) "And just so you know, you're not turning into a mutant... unless you start glowing in the dark—then we might need to call someone." Son: (laughs) "I'm not glowing. Yet."

Father: "Good. I already have enough trouble paying the electric bill—I don't need a human light bulb in the house." (they both laugh) Father (softer tone): "But seriously, this is a big deal. It's okay to feel caught in the middle. Growing up isn't a straight line—it's more like trying to fold a fitted sheet. Nobody really knows what they're doing at first." Son: (chuckling) "That's a terrible example... but also kind of true." Father: "Exactly. And I want you to know something significant: you don't have to figure it all out on your own. I'm here.

Always. Not to lecture, not to give you a list of rules—but to walk with you through all of it. Whenever you want to talk—or even just sit and eat an awkward amount of chips in silence—I'm your guy." Son: "Thanks, Dad. That actually makes me feel better."

Father:

"Anytime, son. Also—chip bags are 70% air and 30% disappointment. Just like my first attempt at parenting. But hey—we're both learning."

Father:

I would like you to know something significant: you don't have to figure it all out on your own. I'm here. Always. Not to lecture, not to give you a list of rules—but to walk with you through all of it. Whenever you want to talk—or even just sit in silence—I'm right here."

Son:

"Thanks, Dad. That really helps."

Temptation Is Real—But So Is God's Strength

Father:

"Let's talk about something important. Do you know how gravity works?"

Son:

"Yeah, it pulls things down to the ground."

Father:

"Exactly. It's constantly pulling—without asking, without warning. Temptation works the same way. Especially with sex, it pulls hard. You don't have to go looking for it—it's already waiting for you: on your phone, at school, online, in your own head.

But here's the good news: just like a plane still flies despite gravity, you can rise above temptation. How? Planes use something more substantial than gravity—the law of lift and thrust. We have something more significant, too: God's Spirit. Romans 8:2 says, 'The law of the Spirit of life in Christ Jesus has set us free from the law of sin and death.' That means, even when temptation feels strong, God's grace is stronger."

The Balloon Analogy: Why Obedience Lifts You Higher

Father:

"Let me paint you a picture. Imagine two balloons.

Now, every day, one balloon gets a little spoonful of sand—just ¼ teaspoon. Not much, right? But over time, it starts to sink. That's what sin does. It weighs us down little by little. One small compromise here. One wrong choice there. And before you know it, you're not flying—you're sinking.

Now, imagine the second balloon. Every time that boy obeys God—even in small things—5ml of helium gets added into his balloon. He chooses to say no to something wrong. He tells the truth. He walks away from temptation. Every act of obedience fills him with God's grace—*helium for the soul.*

For over a month, this balloon has been full of air. It's tied securely. It doesn't go down. In fact, it soars. You place it in water, and it floats. But the sand-filled balloon? That one sinks.

So what's the difference?
What's inside.

If a person can't say no to sin, it's not because they're weak. It's because their balloon is empty of grace. But here's the beautiful part—God gives grace freely. All you have to do is ask."

Father (continued):
"When you feel the pull of temptation, pray right there:

'Jesus, help me. Give me grace right now.'
And you'll feel it—like a gust of wind lifting your balloon. Grace doesn't always make it easy, but it makes it possible."

Joseph's Story: He Ran

Son:
"So... what do I do when the temptation feels stronger than me?"

Father:
"Good question. You're not the first to face that. Remember Joseph? He was a young guy like you. Good-looking. Smart. Faithful. He

worked for a powerful man named Potiphar. But Potiphar's wife tried to seduce him.

She was bold—offering pleasure, safety, and maybe even promotion. But Joseph knew what was at stake. If he gave in, he'd lose the one thing that made his life meaningful—God's presence, the great asset and power that he has.

So what did he do? Did he try to argue with her? Nope.

He ran. Fast. Left his coat behind and everything. That's not weakness—that's wisdom."

Son:
"Like... literally ran?"

Father:
"Yep! And sometimes, that's exactly what you need to do. Delete the app. Shut the screen. Walk out of the room. Don't try to fight fire with bare hands—*flee it*."

Reuben's Story: He Stayed Silent and Lost Everything

Father:
"Now contrast that with Reuben—Joseph's older brother. He gave in to temptation and secretly slept with his father's wife. It seemed like no one noticed. No one said anything.

But years later, when Jacob—his father—was dying and ready to bless his sons, he looked at Reuben and said, 'You will not excel.' Why? Because of that hidden sin. It showed up at the worst possible moment and cost him the blessing of a lifetime.

So remember: sin might feel hidden, but it's never harmless."

Purity: Not About Perfection—It's About Protection

Son:

"So being pure just means never messing up?"

Father:

"Nope. Purity isn't about being perfect. It's about guarding something valuable—God's presence, access to the things of God, your future, your mind, your peace.

When you live a pure life, you sleep better. You think clearer. You avoid shame. And one day, when you look into the eyes of your wife, you'll have nothing to hide. That's a gift you'll both be thankful for."

The Big Questions

Q1: Why should I wait?

Father:

"Because sex isn't just a physical act—it's a soul connection. Every time you give yourself away, you give away part of your heart.

Waiting protects your heart so you can give all of it to the one God made for you."

Q2: What if I already messed up?

Father:
"Then run to Jesus. He doesn't shame you—He restores you. Don't hide. Don't delay. Repent quickly. He'll clean your heart and fill your balloon with grace again."

Q3: What if I do wait?

Father:
"Then you'll walk into marriage with joy, peace, and confidence. No baggage. No regret. Just freedom. And your wife will see you as a man who was faithful even before he met her."

How to Stay Pure – Real, Practical Steps

1. Guard Your Eyes:
"You can't always control what pops up—but you *can* control how long you look. Turn away fast. Delete the app if you need to."

Verse: "Flee youthful lusts..." – 2 Timothy 2:22

2. Don't Believe 'Just Once' Is Harmless:
"That's the hook. One 'just once' turns into a habit. Think of sin like mouldy bread—it doesn't matter if you eat a little or a lot, it still makes you sick."

Real Example:

"Remember James from youth group? One slip turned into a two-year battle. He's healing now, but he says the hardest part was feeling trapped in silence."

3. Use Spiritual Tools:

"When I feel tempted, I speak a verse out loud. Try this one:

> *'I am not my own—I was bought with a price.'*
> *– 1 Corinthians 6:19-20*

I also fast once a week. It tells my body, 'You're not the boss of me.' Try skipping lunch and spending that time praying instead.

And have one person you can text when things get tough. Don't walk this road alone."

Stories That Stick

Joseph:

He ran. He resisted. God honoured him with wisdom, power, marriage, and legacy.

Reuben:

He gave in. Thought it was a secret. Lost everything when it counted most.

Jordan (Real Story):

He started watching porn at 12. Hid it for years. At 19, it nearly ended his engagement. He finally opened up to his dad—and that's when healing began.

Final Words From a Dad Who Loves His Son

Father:

"Son, listen—God made you strong. But He never asked you to do this alone. When temptation hits, ask for grace. Pray, 'Jesus, fill my balloon today.' And He will.

Run from what will destroy you. Fight for what will build you. And never forget—you're not just my son.

You're God's son.

And I'll be walking beside you every step of the way."

Father teachings #11 Father–Mother & Son Dialogue: Nourish, Illuminate, Guard & Grow

Divine Connection & Spiritual Vision

Dad: "Son, when you gave your life to Jesus, the Holy Spirit came into you—your SIM card. Without it, your phone (or life) is useless."

Son: "So the Spirit isn't just inside me, He helps me connect with God?"

Mum: "Yes—and Paul prays in Ephesians 1 that our *'eyes of understanding be enlightened'* so we see Scripture from God's perspective, not just learn facts ."

Reflection Prompt:
- Ask your teen: *When has God's Word felt alive to you—more than just information?*

Spiritual Nutrition

Dad: "Just as you need food to survive physically, you need Scripture to survive in your destiny."

Mum: "Study daily so you know God's voice in decisions. That 'pressing word' will guide you—just like a healthy diet keeps you strong."

Checklist:
- Daily Scripture reading
- Prayer and reflection

- Weekly dad/son or mum/son study time

Biblical Examples & Modern Testimonies from Different Cultures

Dad: "Look at David in the wilderness: he fed on God's Word even under fire."

Mum: "And Daniel in Babylon—he stayed true because he ate the spiritual food from God, even in exile."

Modern Positive Story: A UK father used monthly devotions, invited his son to lead part, then publicly affirmed him after he taught—it sparked leadership in youth group. Similarly, a mother in the US encouraged her daughter to use social media as a platform for sharing her faith, leading to a significant impact on her peers.

Modern Negative Story: A boy left unguided spiritually; in his 20s, he's struggling with identity and purpose—parents wish they'd started EARLIER.

Spotting Subtle Deception: The Guardian Role Dad (quiet voice): "Isaiah 66:2 warns that only the humble who value God's Word are safe from deception. We must be vigilant and guide you in this, son."**Dad (quiet voice):** "Isaiah 66:2 warns that only the humble who value God's Word are safe from deception .

Mum: "Satan slithers in quietly—he used a serpent because it hides. He uses questions like *'Did God really say…?'* to sow doubt."

Son: "So I need to know My Father's real voice to spot illusions?"

Mum: "Exactly. The stronger you feed and see, the less you'll be fooled."

Spiritual "Gym Training"
Dad: "Like physical exercise, spiritual discipline strengthens you. Prayer, Scripture, worship—all build resistance."

Mum: "Even when you don't feel like it—do it anyway. Over time, those distractions won't lure you in."

Exercise Checklist:
- Set spiritual goals
- Use apps/journals/habits trackers
- Celebrate wins and breakthroughs

Testing & Affirmation
Dad: "Every month, we'll have a sit-down. I'll ask: 'What did Ephesians teach you?' or 'How will you guard your heart today?'"

Mum: "If your answers show genuine revelation—not just memorised facts—I'll say: *'We affirm you as a disciple-maker.'* That's your moment of official commissioning."

Interactive Element:
- Journal space: *What question would you ask in our monthly check-in?*

Full-Throttle Modern Battle Tools

Parents today crave help with:

- **Social media boundaries:** Set limits, discuss emoji etiquette, screen time, and online dangers.

- **Peer pressure & identity:** Use Ephesians 6:11 armor-of-God talk to prepare for school tests, friendships, and trends.

- **Mental health support:** Discuss anxiety, loneliness; normalise tough feelings and coping through Scripture.

- **Purity guidance:** Tie biblical wisdom to digital temptations—no shame, just truth & grace.

Reflection Prompts:

- *What triggers you most online?*

- *How can scripture replace that lie?*

- *Who can you call, pray or study Scripture with today?*

Conclusion:
A Legacy Worth Leaving

Parenting a teenage boy today is far from being simple. It can really be overwhelming and unpredictable, and some days, you're just doing your best to keep your head above water.

Maybe he's testing limits, shutting himself away in his room for hours, or having an outburst over something that seems minor to you—but feels massive to him. In those moments, you'll likely ask, *Am I doing enough? Am I even on the right track?*

And when plans fall apart, conversations go sideways, or nothing seems to work, it's easy to feel unsure or like you're failing. But that feeling of uncertainty? It's completely normal. Every parent—no matter how experienced—goes through it, especially when things aren't going as expected. It's all part of the process, and you're not alone. But in those moments, know that you're not alone—what you're doing matters more than you may realize. But in the middle of the chaos, there's something only you can give your son—a legacy built on faith, love, and the wisdom you've gathered from your own life.

As we've explored in this book, guiding your son toward the man God has designed him to be is a journey full of ups and downs. There will be moments of joy and frustration, times when things feel clear, and others when the road ahead feels uncertain. And here's the reality: this journey doesn't have a neat, finished endpoint. It will most likely continue to have changes as your son grows and as life presents new challenges. And that's perfectly okay. Every step, twist, and turn is part of a bigger story that will continue to shape your son and the bond you share with him.

What matters most is that you're present. You must show up every day, even when it's hard, and love him with all the grace and patience you can muster. Things won't always be perfect—and that's alright. Your consistent investment in his life matters because that's what truly shapes him. The faith, values, and love you pour into him now will lay the foundation for the man he'll become tomorrow. And that legacy will last long after his teenage years are behind him.

Keep trusting the process. Trust that God guides you and your son, even when the journey gets tough, or you can't see the next step clearly. Trust that your son is learning more from you than you might realize—by watching you, seeing you live out your faith, and feeling the love and support you offer. That's your legacy—a legacy rooted in faith, nurtured through love, and carried through every high and low of life. It's a legacy that will echo in your son's heart for years to come and will shape the man he will one day be.

Please Leave a Review!

I would be incredibly thankful if you could take just 60 seconds to write a brief review on the platform of purchase, even if it's just a few sentences!

Other Books You'll Love!

1. <u>The Fear of The Lord: How God's Honour Guarantees Your Peace</u>

2. Parenting Teenage Girls for Purpose: Guiding Godly Young Girls to Walk in Charisma, Character, Calling, Life Skills, and Christ-Centered Confidence

3. <u>Raising Teenagers to Choose Wisely: Keeping your Teen Secure in a Big World</u>

4. <u>Spelling one: An Interactive Vocabulary & Spelling Workbook for 5-Year-Olds. *(With Audiobook Lessons)*</u>

5. <u>Spelling Two: An Interactive Vocabulary & Spelling Workbook for 6-Year-Olds. *(With Audiobook Lessons)*</u>

6. <u>Spelling Three: An Interactive Vocabulary & Spelling Workbook for 7-Year-Olds. *(With Audiobook Lessons)*</u>

7. <u>Spelling Four: An Interactive Vocabulary & Spelling Workbook for 8-Year-Olds. *(With Audiobook Lessons)*</u>

8. _Spelling Five: An Interactive Vocabulary & Spelling Workbook for 9-Year-Olds. (With Audiobook Lessons)_

9. _Spelling Six: An Interactive Vocabulary & Spelling Workbook for 10 & 11 Years Old. (With Audiobook Lessons)_

10. _Spelling Seven: An Interactive Vocabulary & Spelling Workbook for 12-14 Years-Old. (With Audiobook Lessons)_

11. _Raising Boys in Today's Digital World: Proven Positive Parenting Tips for Raising Respectful, Successful, and Confident Boys_

12. _Raising Girls in Today's Digital World: Proven Positive Parenting Tips for Raising Respectful, Successful, and Confident Girls_

13. _Raising Kids in Today's Digital World: Proven Positive Parenting Tips for Raising Respectful, Successful, and Confident Kids_

14. _The Child Development and Positive Parenting Master Class 2-in-1 Bundle: Proven Methods for Raising Well-Behaved and Intelligent Children, with Accelerated Learning Methods_

15. _Parenting Teens in Today's Challenging World 2-in-1 Bundle: Proven Methods for Improving Teenager's Behaviour with Positive Parenting and Family Communication_

16. Life Strategies for Teenagers: Positive Parenting, Tips and Understanding Teens for Better Communication and a Happy Family

17. Parenting Teen Girls in Today's Challenging World: Proven Methods for Improving Teenager's Behaviour with Whole Brain Training

18. Parenting Teen Boys in Today's Challenging World: Proven Methods for Improving Teenager's Behaviour with Whole Brain Training

19. 101 Tips For Helping With Your Child's Learning: Proven Strategies for Accelerated Learning and Raising Smart Children Using Positive Parenting Skills

20. 101 Tips for Child Development: Proven Methods for Raising Children and Improving Kids Behavior with Whole Brain Training

21. Financial Tips to Help Kids: Proven Methods for Teaching Kids Money Management and Financial Responsibility

22. Healthy Habits for Kids: Positive Parenting Tips for Fun Kids Exercises, Healthy Snacks, and Improved Kids Nutrition

23. Mini Habits for Happy Kids: Proven Parenting Tips for Positive Discipline and Improving Kids' Behavior

24. Good Habits for Healthy Kids 2-in-1 Combo Pack: Proven Positive Parenting Tips for Improving Kid's Fitness and Children's Behavior

25. T Raising Teenagers to Choose Wisely: Keeping your Teen Secure in a Big World

26. Tips for #CollegeLife: Powerful College Advice for Excelling as a College Freshman

27. The Career Success Formula: Proven Career Development Advice and Finding Rewarding Employment for Young Adults and College Graduates

28. The Motivated Young Adult's Guide to Career Success and Adulthood: Proven Tips for Becoming a Mature Adult, Starting a Rewarding Career, and Finding Life Balance

29. Bedtime Stories for Kids: Short Funny Stories and poems Collection for Children and Toddlers

30. Guide for Boarding School Life

Your Free Gift!

As a way of saying thank you for Your purchase, I have included a gift that you can download at TCEC publishing .com

References

Blight, W. (2014). *Trials come so that... The Triangle Tribune*, 16(5), 6B.

Boggs, K. (2014). *When a child dies. The Triangle Tribune*, 16(15), 6B.

"Consider it pure joy, my brothers and sisters, whenever you face trials of many kinds..." – *Bible Inspirations*. Retrieved from https://bibleinspirations.org/consider-it-pure-joy-my-brothers-and-sisters-whenever-you-face-trials-of-many-kinds/

"For I know the plans I have for you," declares the LORD, "plans to prosper you and not to harm you, plans to give you hope and a future." (2021). *Florida Times-Union*, B-6.

Fashion trends – Help Youth Cope. Retrieved from https://helpyouthcope.org/tag/fashion-trends/

Fighter Verses. *Set 5 Week 34.* Retrieved from https://www.fighterverses.com/blog/tags/set-5-week-34

God pursues intimacy with Abraham – Two Journeys. Retrieved from https://twojourneys.org/sermons/series/genesis/god-pursues-intimacy-with-abraham/

How to help a teen with depression: What you need to know. Retrieved from https://bhouses.net/blog/how-to-help-a-teen-with-depression/

How to identify your calling – The Purposed Family. Retrieved from https://thepurposedfamily.com/es/bible-verse-blogs/how-to-identify-your-calling/

Johnson, D. C. (2023). *GCM: Generations in community on mission: A theoretical framework for intergenerational disciples on mission.* Retrieved from https://digitalcommons.georgefox.edu/cgi/viewcontent.cgi?article=1582&context=dmin

Jones, K. *Kelly Jones Photography.* Retrieved from http://www.kellyjonesphotography.com

Mall, A. (2020). "As for me and my house." *Journal of Popular Music Studies*, 32(1), 10. https://doi.org/10.1525/jpms.2020.32.1.10

Malachi 4:6. Retrieved from https://biblehub.com/malachi/4-6.htm

"The righteous person may have many troubles, but the Lord delivers him from them all…" — Psalm 34:19. Retrieved from https://clicktotweet.com/mv5L2

Sharpen somebody. (2024). *Jackson Advocate*, 86(30), 9A.

Thomas, D. (2024). A more profound legacy than hard work. *The Christian Century*, 141(4), 30–31.

Unless the Lord builds the house, those who make it labour in vain. Retrieved from https://www.hitched.ie/wedding-planning/readings/unless-the-lord-builds-the-house-those-who-build-it-labour-in-vain_625.htm

Your face, Lord, I will seek – Blessed Be Boutique. Retrieved from https://blessedbeboutique.com/blogs/news/your-face-lord-i-will-seek

Whitefield, G. (2024). *The great duty of family religion.* https://doi.org/10.3735/9781961844117.book-part-056

Williams, D. (2020). A conversation with... Darren Williams, Ph.D. *Products Finishing*, 84(5), 52.

www.ingramcontent.com/pod-product-compliance
Lightning Source LLC
Chambersburg PA
CBHW052022070526
44584CB00016B/1867